Redefining Competency Based Education

Redefining Competency Based Education

Competence for Life

Nina Jones Morel and Bruce Griffiths

BEP BUSINESS EXPERT PRESS

Redefining Competency Based Education: Competence for Life

Copyright © Business Expert Press, LLC, 2018.

First published in 2018 by
Business Expert Press, LLC
222 East 46th Street, New York, NY 10017
www.businessexpertpress.com

ISBN-13: 978-1-63157-899-1 (paperback)
ISBN-13: 978-1-63157-900-4 (e-book)

Business Expert Press Human Resource Management and Organizational Behavior Collection

Collection ISSN: 1946-5637 (print)
Collection ISSN: 1946-5645 (electronic)

Cover and interior design by Exeter Premedia Services Private Ltd., Chennai, India

First edition: 2018

10 9 8 7 6 5 4 3 2 1

Printed in the United States of America.

Abstract

Redefining Competency-Based Education will provide readers with an expanded definition of career competence that is based on actual employer hiring and promotion requirements and that can be used to enhance current university curricula to better prepare students for work, and for life. Readers will learn how private sector competency models have evolved to be current best practice in human resource departments in defining criteria for use in hiring, promoting, and training talent. Current industry competency models will be contrasted with classic university models to document an academic preference for technical career preparation that historically has provided less attention to the so-called *soft skills* valued by the industry. These industry-valued skills include competence in areas such as communication, team, multitasking, and problem-solving. In the world of work, these are the competencies that are proven to provide significant advantage in career success. Techniques for measuring, and developing, *soft skills* are explained, and two examples of universities who have successfully implemented these concepts are provided. Questions for reflection will help readers review and summarize important content in each chapter.

Keywords

ability, assessment, behaviors, business, career, coaching, college, company, competency, development, education, feedback, human resource, knowledge, learning, model, organization, performance, process, professional, role, skills, student, success, technology, talent, university

Contents

Foreword

In a world where the value of a college education is constantly questioned, universities have been challenged to ensure curricula are relevant to our digital, global, and dynamic world. The increasing competition from for-profit organizations paired with the restrictions of a traditional four-year degree create a pressing need to dramatically change how we educate and prepare students in the Age of Innovation. Morel and Griffiths provide a framework to enhance that educational approach by emphasizing the importance of not just *knowing*. Now more than ever, today's graduates need to be content knowledgeable, but also prepared to apply their knowledge and *do*. Gone are the days where people come to universities to learn basic knowledge and passively develop competencies such as critical thinking, learning agility and creativity. Universities must embrace their role of holistically and intentionally developing these competencies so graduates are prepared for a successful and meaningful life. *Redefining Competency Based Education - Competence for Life* guides higher education to help spark that change. This book is a necessary reading for those of us in academia and relevant to those who work in K-12 education as well. Thanks to Nina and Bruce for authenticating this important educational approach that will shape how we *do* moving forward.

Dr. Rodney Rogers, PhD
President
Bowling Green State University
Bowling Green. Ohio

Acknowledgments

The most profound experience in my professional life was when I came into contact with the practice, competencies, and profession of coaching. But, little did I know that my passion and understanding of coaching would lead me to many dynamic, innovative individuals who were seeking ways to develop competencies in adult students—chief among them Bruce Griffiths. I am truly grateful for his professional partnership, as we and other colleagues have sought to develop new practices around the development of competencies for life in higher education.

This book would not have been possible without the support of my husband David Morel and our children Rachel, Logan, Grant, Connor, and Chandler. This family is unfailingly supportive, no matter what project I undertake.

Undying gratitude is due my colleagues in the College of Professional Studies who do this hard work day after day. I especially want to thank my colleagues April Jarnagin for her editing and reference-checking and Kelli Bratton and Micheal Cauley for reading the manuscript for clarity and accuracy. Thanks also to Gail Walraven for her meticulous *first read* proofing that made everything so much better!

Nina Jones Morel

I have been incubating the idea for a book like this since leaving my graduate program for the world of work some years ago. One of my initial responsibilities in the corporate world was to manage one of America's first assessment centers, and my orientation to that classic process was to be personally assessed against a model set of dimensions correlated with success as a manager. It was a dramatic exposure to a whole new, and very scientific, way to define and measure competence. I immediately saw a need in higher education to at least expose students to this model. So, my first acknowledgment is to my wonderful collaborator, Dr. Nina Morel, for making this happen by taking the lead in writing this book, bringing her enthusiasm for the topic, and her stories and experience from successful application of these ideas at Lipscomb University.

Thanks go also to my better half, Gail Walraven, who gave the manuscript an initial detailed read and offered innumerable improvements. Gail's support in this, and in life, makes all things possible for me. And, as I wrote this book, my three sons unknowingly provided feedback and confirmation of our ideas as they finished college, prepared for, and entered the world of work. We have had many, many discussions about their career challenges and successes. All of these conversations have informed, and confirmed, our central thesis. So, thanks to Kellen, Dustin, and Case!

My brother, Keith Griffiths, also donated time to read and suggest improvements. His experience as a writer, journalist, and professional editor is much appreciated. Again, thanks to all who helped make this happen. It does take a village.

Bruce Griffiths

Introduction

A classic television commercial from the 1970s and 1980s shows two people separately enjoying a snack, blissfully unaware of the other. In each version of this ad, they clumsily run into each other and one says, "Hey, you got your chocolate in my peanut butter!" The other replies "And you got your peanut butter in my chocolate!" Inevitably, they each take a bite of their new snack and realize something great has happened.

In that spirit, we, authors from two different disciplines enjoying our peanut butter and chocolate, offer this book to practitioners in the fields of higher education and of business. For too long, we have attempted to solve our problems separately, never quite recognizing what can happen when our worlds collide. Both worlds are now facing unprecedented challenges. Employers are finding it increasingly difficult to find the skills they need among recent college graduates. Higher education is struggling to stay relevant, affordable, and equitable. Both are trying to survive and thrive in the face of global and technological shifts occurring on an unprecedented scale.

While a bachelor's degree is still considered a necessary step to career progression and a way to narrow the applicant pool, the gap between what organizations need and the skills and abilities a bachelor's degree actually provides is growing (Friedman 2016). As more technical skills become automated, employers are placing increased importance on the interpersonal and team abilities of the college graduates they hire. This gap between what businesses want and what universities provide has grown as the workplace becomes increasingly digital, global, and millennial. The Washington Post reported that "*nearly a third of business leaders and technology analysts express 'no confidence' that education and job training in the U.S. will evolve rapidly enough to match the next decade's labor market demands ...*" (Paquette 2017). The competency-based education (CBE) movement seeks to provide a more practical, outcome-focused curriculum in many universities, but has not yet had much national impact on the development of the soft skills and cross-cutting competencies needed in a world where content knowledge can be obsolete in a couple of years. While not abandoning technical and content knowledge that classic degrees must continue to provide, this book will propose a new path to develop *competencies for life* that has been, and is being, created in some innovative universities and organizations.

The authors define *competence for life* as those skills, historically referred to as soft skills, that are non-cognitive, interpersonal, or intrapersonal in nature. They include social skills, coping skills, adaptability, and professional habits of mind that are broadly applicable across many jobs and professions over the lifespan of an individual. Indeed, these are the same skills that lead to success in personal and civic life, as well as professional careers. While widely touted as necessary for professional success, these competencies have not been explicitly taught or measured in traditional higher education in the last 100 years. The gap between what schools teach and what employers say they want from graduates is largely due to the inability of colleges and universities to ensure that graduates' non-cognitive skills consistently match the technical skills that are required to pass courses and graduate from programs.

This book explores this classic gap from the two perspectives of its authors. As an industry consultant, Bruce Griffiths has been on the receiving side of this talent equation for over 40 years, helping organizations select, hire, and promote talent, often directly from university campuses. He has seen first-hand the strengths and deficiencies of college degrees as young chemical engineers come into a sales and marketing function in a large, multi-national company, or a graduate-level physicist suddenly finds herself in a supervisory role in a high-technology firm.

By contrast, Nina Morel has spent her career on the delivery side, preparing students for this world of work. She has been on the leading edge of understanding just how to improve the college experience to make sure graduates hit the ground running in organizations. Her industry partnerships have informed innovative changes in how the college she leads now thinks about, and prepares, students to step into that first, or next, job.

Both authors' interests in bridging this gap between organizational talent needs and educational preparation actually reaches back decades. Bruce's own dual career trajectories fueled his personal passion for this topic. He was outwardly prepared for two very different roles, in two very different career contexts, by two very different institutions. His first career began when he accepted a scholarship to pursue a BS in Marine Engineering from the U.S. Coast Guard Academy. This very specialized technical degree provided the content knowledge needed to serve in the Coast Guard (especially at sea where he swung an arc with a sextant to help navigate a ship around the world), and his training as a cadet at the academy (resulting in a commission as an Ensign in the U.S. Coast Guard) ostensibly prepared him to lead.

After serving five years of active duty in the Coast Guard, Bruce re-tooled himself as an industrial/organizational (I/O) psychologist with an MS in Applied Psychology from San Diego State University. This graduate degree provided a deep understanding of the content of I/O psychology he needed as he launched into a career as an internal and then external I/O consultant and entrepreneur. Looking back on his 27-year career in the Coast Guard and Coast Guard reserve, where he retired as a Captain in 1993, and his 40-year career as an I/O psychologist, he knows that his formal training fell short, both undergraduate and graduate. Neither academic institution prepared him for leadership or consulting roles as they over-emphasized the importance of technical content (hard skills) and under-emphasized or ignored the importance of the absolutely essential *soft* skills that differentiate high performers.

In the case of the Coast Guard, the most instructive period of Bruce's career was actually a tour as an exchange officer on a U.S. Navy destroyer. Here he learned true leadership competence from an outstanding role model, his commanding officer. And, while life lessons can provide dramatic instruction, there is no reason that good leadership competencies could not have been introduced as part of his undergraduate education. Likewise, those competencies necessary to start and build a consulting practice could have been included in his graduate program.

Nina Morel's first educational experiences were the exact opposite. She graduated from a small, traditional liberal arts college with degrees in history and English, and a minor in German—a path that seemed to lead only to graduate school. And, when the next step, law school, was on the horizon, she realized she did not want to be a lawyer. She wanted to use the competencies learned in history and English to do something else—to write, organize, create, and persuade. This led to a winding path as a college career placement director, non-profit communications coordinator, legislative lobbyist, and finally into the profession of education, where those competencies and others were honed and developed, but not in graduate school. Although her master's degree and doctorate at a large state university were rigorous, the main skills she learned were to be a better researcher and writer—skills that were only moderately necessary in her career as a school district administrator. However, it was in this role that she developed her passion for improving the professional learning of adults and became curious about how to best accomplish that goal.

After teaching at the middle and high-school level and realizing that neither her education courses nor professional development workshops developed teaching skills, Nina was looking for a better way to help develop the teachers who reported to her. Instructional coaching seemed to be the answer. For the first time, she applied a learning method that really resonated with adults—a method that allowed them to drive their own learning. And, for the first time, Nina experienced competency-based learning—learning to coach from a school that emphasized *performance* of the recognized International Coach Federation coaching competencies (mainly soft skills) over the *academic knowledge* of those skills. The gap between knowing and doing was bridged with observation and feedback in her coaching curriculum.

Coaching drew her to the university, where she encountered a competency and assessment model created by Bruce Griffiths. Using that assessment model of competencies, she and her team crafted a learning model to develop adult students' personal and leadership competencies that are valued by the workplace.

Both Bruce and Nina experienced the best of American higher education over many decades. Their personal and professional experiences led them to explore and develop competencies that have brought them satisfying and impactful careers. But, the stakes have gotten higher. Fewer companies are willing to take a risk on a student whose abilities are unproven. Students are struggling to find ways to communicate what they can do based on what they have learned in school. Higher education is struggling to find ways to provide value to students that can translate into a more satisfying and successful career.

A growing movement in education and industry seeks to address the competency gap by combining what organizations know about competence (i.e., competency models) into the higher education curriculum. This shift in emphasis by higher education is now more important than ever as the pace of change accelerates and many technical degrees must come with a *use by* date as they face obsolescence in years, not decades. Graduates need to *learn how to learn* so that they can stay relevant over potential decades of their careers. Employers are at risk of being overwhelmed by the complexity and change that technology and global challenges bring. How can education and industry partner to solve the mutual challenge of a workforce prepared to handle complex human interactions, curate massive information, and make decisions based on data and knowledge of human propensities? This book provides some answers.

In the following pages, you will learn:

- What competence is, and how industry defines it.
- What the competence gap is, and how education providers are prepared to fill it.
- How to measure and develop competence for life.
- How two universities have already made great strides toward developing competence for life.
- What employers and educators need to do to close the gap.

CHAPTER 1

Defining Competence for Life

Humans do things, and they typically do them well or not-so-well. Most of the motivation for things we do is to survive or to thrive. We work, we eat, we create shelter, we love, we fight, we make art, we rear children, we form communities, we worship, and we celebrate. In each of these things we do in life, we have roles. Our roles are economic, civic, familial, and personal. We are parents, children, spouses, citizens, chiefs, artists, doctors, lawyers, bricklayers, plumbers—sometimes many of these things at once. For each of these roles that we perform, there are specific knowledge, skills, abilities, and attitudes that are necessary to perform the tasks assigned to those roles. These are competencies. This has not changed over millennia. What has changed is the complexity surrounding each of these basic human occupations and the knowledge, skills, abilities, and attitudes required to be competent in them.

In the world of human resources (HR), a differentiation is typically made between general competencies (often called soft skills) and technical competencies. This differentiation is not always clear, because some *technical competencies* of the past, like using a computer and basic software, have become so ubiquitous that they are now considered general baseline competencies, even though they are not soft skills. Within the general competencies, however, there is a group of skills and attitudes that are becoming more and more important. They are called by various names—soft skills, 21st-century skills, non-cognitive skills, cross-cutting skills—skills that the authors consider *competencies for life*.

Competencies for life (soft skills) prepare one for roles in all aspects of life, not just the workplace. But more importantly, they are useful over the span of a long career, no matter the context, and become even more important as workers advance from frontline to leadership roles.

In the not-so-distant past, a person could personally perform every role in the production of a product or the delivery of a service. A carpenter could cut a tree and build a cabinet that could be sold directly to a consumer. Today, the wood may come from several different countries, the hardware from others. The cabinet might be made in a factory by 30 different hands, or by robots. Other individuals would handle digital and analog advertising, website, credit card payments, packing, shipping, distribution, sales, and delivery. The reality is that, for the vast majority of us, we work in the context of an organization. Few people get to enjoy creating a product or process from idea to execution all by themselves; most of us work in teams. The workplace dictates that the *real* definition of *competence* derives from the demands of a communal context. The workplace is typically a structured *team,* with production and cooperation demands, requiring much more than a specific knowledge base. To be successful, we must arrive to work on time, communicate, solve problems, be efficient with resources, be creative and take risks; in short, we must exercise what are called soft skills. These skillsets are *absolutely essential* to providing value in an organizational context.

There is a long-standing and dramatic difference between how academia categorizes *needed job and life competence,* and how it is categorized by business organizations, which make up 85 percent of the current workforce.[1] Most universities view the competencies required to succeed in a career in the context of narrowly defined specific knowledge (and skills) set in classic content disciplines. These most popularly include[2]:

- Computer Science
- Communications
- Government or Political Science
- Business
- Economics
- English Language or Literature
- Psychology
- Nursing
- Chemical Engineering
- Biology

While many of these academic and professional disciplines have articulated competencies and some have industry-required performance or proficiency testing to hold students accountable for demonstrating outcomes, their actual overall model of competence, if there is one, often does not encompass all of the skillsets needed for a particular role as defined by the business organizations that might employ their graduates. Most academic disciplines (with the exception of professional disciplines such as education, nursing, and engineering) are not and were never designed to correlate to one specific role within an organization. A biology major may go into research, teaching, medicine, or a host of business applications. An English major may become a journalist, teacher, technical writer, novelist, lobbyist, or continue on to graduate school to study law, business, or literature.

Of course, business and higher education have two different purposes. The primary purpose of business is the business; human development, while important to the bottom line, is secondary. For higher education, the business is human development, but a second purpose is the vocational success of the student. It goes without saying that earning a college degree does more than just prepare graduates for a career. A good college experience broadens knowledge and perspective, reinforces life-long learning, creates a network of friends and colleagues, and provides a broader context to understand the world. But if you Google *Why go to college*, the top response is *you will earn, on average, $1 million more over the arc of your career* than a high-school graduate. People go to college for many reasons, but chief among them is to prepare for a career—to be competent in a chosen profession.

Employers have a different perspective of competence. While a university may consider a student competent in history, translating those competencies to a business setting may be as difficult as translating a different language. Most large and successful companies have sophisticated competency models, in which they identify the knowledge, skills, abilities, and attitudes needed to perform each role within the organization. Most universities (with the exception of some burgeoning competency-based programs, which will be discussed later) do not. Instead of competencies, universities have courses of study, usually confined to academic disciplines, that include teaching objectives and student outcomes, often assessed by a test or project. Although writing a research paper might correlate to written communication skills in a company competency model, there are few crosswalks between the two. Many competencies, especially those most desired by companies, are not addressed in college syllabi at all; if they are, it is not in language that connects to traditional corporate competency models.

Most employers that have a competency model have a slate of general competencies, often related to corporate values, that are required by all employees, as well as other competencies that are job specific. To advance in leadership, mastery of the core general competencies of an organization is vital. To get an idea of how employers view competencies, let us take a look inside some of the historically most admired companies in America and see how they define the knowledge and skills needed to excel in their organizations.

Dell Computers

Dell Inc. is a multinational computer technology company located in Round Rock, Texas. Employing more than 100,000 individuals, it is one of the largest technology companies in the world. Dell manufactures, sells, repairs, and supports personal computers (PCs) and other electronics.

Dell's talent development programs are based on the Dell competency model, which was created through analysis of 360-degree feedback data, performance appraisals, derailment studies (of those who fail or plateau in their jobs), strategic organizational requirements, and benchmarking data. These competencies were shared among high-performing leaders and identified core success factors across business units and specific functions.

When applied to relevant HR tools and processes, these competencies are integrated into an adopted career development model that assists individuals in developing their careers (Table 1.1).

Table 1.1 Dell Inc. Competencies

Entry-level requirements For leadership positions:	• Functional or technical skills • Integrity and trust • Intellectual horsepower • Business acumen • Command skills

Additional competencies Identified as success factors for leaders:	• Priority setting • Problem-solving • Drive for results • Building effective teams • Developing direct reports • Customer focus • Organization agility • Learning on the fly • Dealing with ambiguity

Disney Consumer Products

Disney Consumer Products and Interactive Media (DCPI) is a segment and subsidiary of the Walt Disney Company that merchandises the Disney brand and properties through various content divisions.

Disney Consumer Products has used a universal custom competency model with 23 competencies clustered into seven areas (Table 1.2).

Table 1.2 Disney Consumer Products

Cluster	Competency
Leadership	• Vision • Influence
Professional mastery	• High personal standards • Functional or technical skills • Learning capacity • Client service orientation
Personal ability	• Adaptability or composure • Energy or stamina • Independence • Self-awareness
Communication	• Informal • Formal • Written • Conflict resolution
Disney team player	• Disney knowledge • Team player • Cultural sensitivity
Resource management	• Task management • People management • Problem-solving or decision-making
Managing the business	• Creativity • Entrepreneurship • Strategic business management

Hewlett-Packard

The Hewlett-Packard Company (HP) is an American multinational information technology company headquartered in Palo Alto, California. It developed and provided a wide variety of hardware components, as well as software and related services to consumers, small- and medium-sized businesses and large enterprises, including customers in government, health, and education sectors.

Historically, HP has used several different consulting organizations and approaches to provide them with leadership development (competency) solutions. However, they are not integrated or applied system-wide. The only system-wide product has been *The HP Way*, which is their value system. A frequently used leadership model at HP is taken from Maynard Leigh Associates, who pioneered the use of theater techniques in business and who had already provided presentation and other interpersonal skills development for the company. HP adopted the seven *I*s leadership model featured in Leigh and Maynard's book, *The Perfect Leader*:

While not technically a competency approach, HP's values are easily translated into competency language. For example, initiative converts directly to the *initiative* competency and also requires elements of *assertiveness* and *self-confidence* that are found in many traditional competency models.

Table 1.3 Hewlett-Packard Competency Model[3]

Competency	Definition
1 Insight	Developing acute awareness of people and situations
2 Initiative	Direct action to expand personal resources
3 Involvement	Producing great team performance, by engaging people in the process
4 Improvisation	Responding creatively to change and thinking spontaneously
5 Inspiration	Living the values and inspiring performance in others
6 Individuality	Personal leadership qualities and style
7 Implementation	Making it happen

Procter & Gamble

Procter & Gamble Co. (P&G) is an American multinational consumer goods corporation headquartered in downtown Cincinnati, Ohio. It was founded in 1837 by British–American William Procter and Irish–American James Gamble. P&G primarily specializes in a wide range of cleaning agents, personal care, and hygienic products. The company continues to be on multiple lists of most respected global organizations. Their competency model is integrated into HR processes system-wide.

Table 1.4 P&G Competency Model[4]

1	Power of minds	
	Thinks and acts decisively	Integrates knowledge or thinks strategically
		Analyzes information or solves problems
		Uses judgment
		Makes timely decisions
	Leverages mastery	Applies mastery
		Understands the business
		Understands the organization
		Possesses professional or technical mastery
	Innovates and reapplies	Innovates holistically
		Creates
		Improves continually
		Reapplies
2	Power of people	
	Leads	Envisions
		Engages
		Energizes
		Enables
		Executes
	Builds diverse, collaborative relationships	Is inclusive
		Collaborates
		Partners externally
		Builds networks
		Respects others
	Grows capability	Learns continually
		Anticipates capability gaps
		Develops others
		Improves systems

3	Power of agility	
	In touch	Listens to understand
		Connects
		Focuses externally
		Turns insights into action
		Is aware
		Possesses self-awareness
	Embraces change	Is open to change
		Initiates change
		Is flexible or adaptable
		Is versatile
	Operates with discipline	Focuses on results
		Is accountable
		Has a scarcity mindset
		Plans and follows through
		Focuses on priorities

Office of Personnel Management

While most college graduates end up working in the private sector, millions will end up employed by city, county, state, and federal entities. The U.S. Office of Personnel Management (OPM) has produced a representative, and respected, public sector leadership model that, once again, reflects the importance of soft skills in defining the ideal leader in the federal workforce. Their model also proves the point that exceptional leadership looks very similar whether you are leading a business, university, or the Parks and Recreation department at a city.

Table 1.5 OPM Leadership Competency Model

OPM Leadership competency model
Leading change   • Creativity and innovation   • External awareness   • Flexibility

- Resilience
- Strategic thinking
- Vision

Leading people
- Conflict management
- Leveraging diversity
- Developing others
- Team building

Results-driven
- Accountability
- Customer service
- Decisiveness
- Entrepreneurship
- Problem-solving
- Technical credibility

Business acumen
- Financial management
- Human capital management
- Technology management

Building coalitions
- Partnering
- Political savvy
- Influencing or negotiating

Fundamental competencies
- Interpersonal skills
- Oral communication
- Integrity or honesty
- Written communication
- Continual learning
- Public service motivation

Best Practices and Benchmark Summary

Even in these few examples, some commonalities begin to emerge. Research reveals that the following competencies are the most common across benchmark models.

It is easy to see from these examples that, when you leave a college campus for a business or public sector job, competence means something dramatically different from the technical and academic competencies most colleges teach and assess. Of course, these respected business organizations do recognize the need for technical competence, but they have learned from decades of research and experience that employees who rise to the top of their fields, both technically and in leadership roles, are proficient in a much broader set of competencies. Given the rapidly changing digital world we now live in, with many academic degrees having an increasingly shorter shelf life, the need for soft skills competencies and life-long learning competencies like *Learning Agility and Adaptability/ Change Management* becomes even more important.

Table 1.6 Competency Themes

Most frequent benchmark competency
1. Adaptability (change mastery)
2. Coaching and counseling (talent management)
3. Creativity
4. Customer orientation
5. High standards
6. Influence
7. Learning agility
8. Mission focus
9. Organizing and planning
10. Problem-solving and decision-making
11. Results orientation
12. Strategic thinking
13. Team management
14. Team player
15. Functional or technical expertise
16. Visioning

Businesses necessarily define competence in the practical terms of performance and behavior—how you show up every day and what you do. Their competitive world is defined by performance, and any shortfall can be an existential threat. So, many of the classic academic measures of success, like ability to correctly answer multiple choice tests, or even express yourself in a short answer or essay format to prove competence, are not necessarily correlated with selling an idea in a corporate meeting, or handling a difficult coworker, or quickly solving a guest's problem in a hospitality setting. It is true that case studies and group projects can provide analogs for future business situations, but without explicit criteria and objective feedback, these exercises have limited transferability. And, as shall be seen next, businesses tend to define competence not through knowledge or intention, but through performance and behavior.

Best Practice Business Definition of Competence

Despite lingering academic debate around definitions,[5] HR professionals concur that a competency serves to connect various historical influences into a single construct, with the *primary definitional element being a behavioral or performance description.*[6] Thus, an individual competency describes a specific set of behaviors or performance indicators associated with a facet of exceptional performance in an organizational role. Each competency reflects a unique combination of knowledge, skills, abilities, and other factors that are driven and influenced by multiple traits and motivations, ultimately manifesting themselves in skillful behavior. A competency model refers to a complete set, or collection, of different competencies that are applicable to a single organization, or more generically, to every organization. Ultimately, competence is manifested in explicit *behaviors* (what you do and how you show up) and *performance* (decisions, actions, and results), while *intent* and *potential* are part of the much more complex, and largely unseen, world of values, traits, and motivations (the *O* in the classic KSAOs—*Knowledge, Skills, Abilities, and Other*).

Active listening is an example of a competency that appears in many models. The definition includes behaviors such as eye contact, head nodding, verbal affirmations, smiles, and accurate paraphrasing or

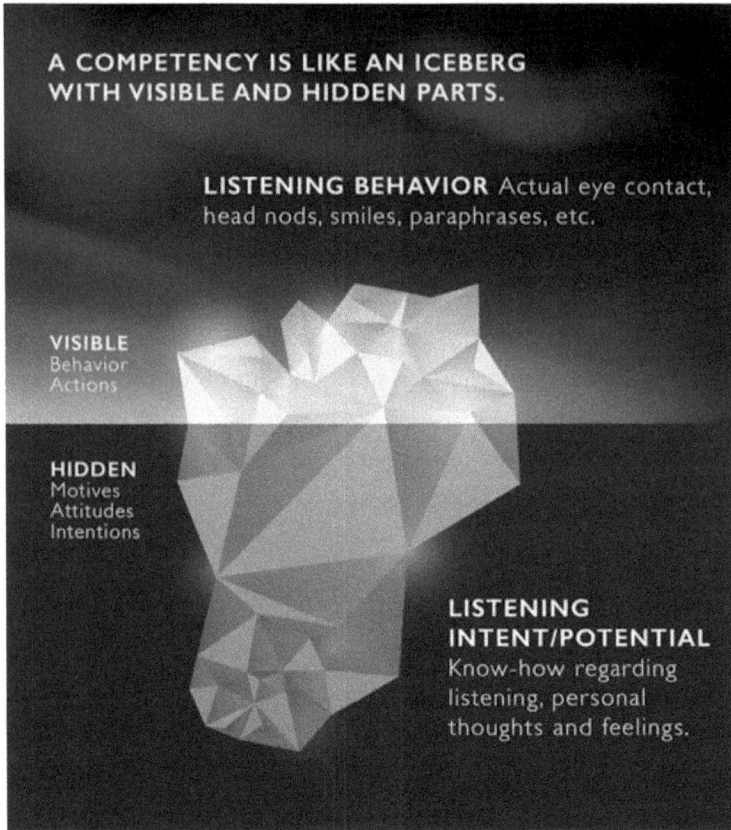

A COMPETENCY IS LIKE AN ICEBERG
WITH VISIBLE AND HIDDEN PARTS.

LISTENING BEHAVIOR Actual eye contact,
head nods, smiles, paraphrases, etc.

VISIBLE
Behavior
Actions

HIDDEN
Motives
Attitudes
Intentions

LISTENING
INTENT/POTENTIAL
Know-how regarding
listening, personal
thoughts and feelings.

Figure 1.1 A simple representation of the concept of competency

summarizing. How one is judged in this competency includes knowing how to listen, and also having the motivation to listen. (Do I value other people's opinions? Am I curious about their experiences and feelings?) While active listening may be a globally applicable concept, the types of behavior that illustrate effective performance have a cultural context that must be factored into local behavioral definitions. For example, in some cultures, listening is important, but looking directly at those in positions of higher authority is considered disrespectful.

Comprehensive competency models offer an integrating framework that provides an essential foundation for key HR processes and a complete menu of dimensions that can be sorted for individual organizational roles and levels. Figure 1.2 shows one commercially available competency model that includes 41 competencies distributed into seven clusters.[7]

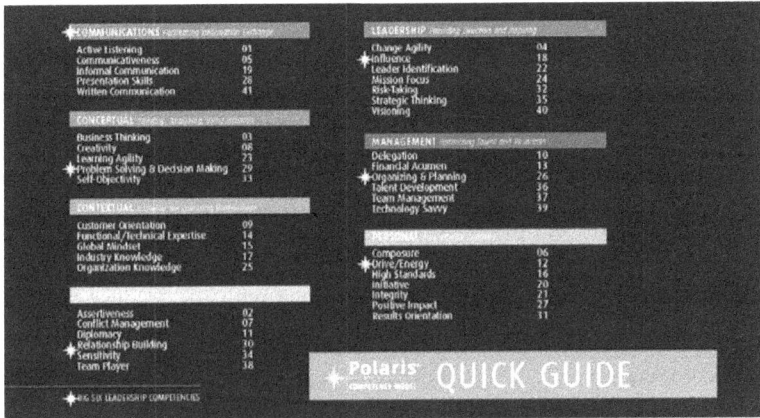

Figure 1.2 Organization Systems International Competency Model

Competencies for the Future

Just as many of the competencies required by the industrial age differed from those of the agricultural age, the future will require adjusted models and benchmarks. Our current age can be summed up in one phrase: accelerating change. We face an increasingly digital, millennial (or younger), and global world with growing climate and resource challenges. This historic nexus of factors is often described by business leaders as a VUCA world—an acronym coined from the military that stands for *volatile, uncertain, changing, and ambiguous.*

This has led to an increased emphasis on selecting for, and developing, classic competencies like:

- *Change agility*
- *Learning agility*
- *Strategic thinking*
- *Global mindset*
- *Communicativeness*
- *Creativity*

The future will probably also demand new hybrid competencies like *collaborative mindset* or *project management* to reflect the reality of this VUCA world. *Sustainability acumen* is another future competency that some organizations are now advertising in their models as a necessary ingredient in current leadership thinking. In a world with growing population and shrinking natural resources, more and more leaders are recognizing the need to conserve and diversify if they expect to thrive in the future.

Competency models are not static. Over time, businesses have seen that certain competencies that were once considered technical or specialized have now become necessary for all employees. Other technical competencies have become obsolete along with the technology that required them. Less volatile, but often more difficult to acquire, are soft skill competencies. So, at the same time that businesses must continue to upgrade their models so that they hire for and train the competencies that reflect current realities, higher education must broaden its definition of professional competency.

Questions for Reflection

- Discuss the differences between traditional academic views and business views of competence.
- Beyond the expertise granted in a specific degree (e.g., Mechanical Engineering, Nursing, Accounting, etc.), what are five or six specific additional competencies that businesses have historically specifically identified as absolutely necessary for success?
- How is competence most practically defined in business and government today (knowledge, skill, ability, personality, and values)?
- Consider competency requirements in the next few decades. What will stay the same? What will change?

CHAPTER 2

Closing the Gap Between What Employers Want and What Higher Education Provides

As we have seen, industry defines competence as specific knowledge, skills, abilities, and attitudes that are necessary to perform the tasks assigned to specific roles within an organization. All one has to do is compare an HR magazine to a higher education journal to see that employers and universities approach the path to competency with profoundly different language, structure, and assessment.

The term competency is largely absent from one place that soft skills should be taught: the general education curriculum. Students learn many *cross-cutting skills* (another term for soft skills) in good general education programs, but often do not have the language to translate what they have learned to a business setting. It is not surprising, given their different goals and organizational structure, that employers focus mainly on meeting general and specific roles within an organization, and universities focus on academic or technical discipline-specific outcomes. More specifically, employers tend to focus on *performance* of a competency, while higher education focuses on domain or discipline *knowledge* that should lead to competent performance. Today, sophisticated employers systematically assess performance in realistic settings. Universities continue to assess academic outcomes primarily through tests, presentations, and written reports. Personal and leadership attributes are assessed through extracurricular activities or informal interactions with faculty and peers. This has led to a gap between what employers want and what higher education has seen as its mission to train students to do.

For generations, society has taken for granted that the job of post-secondary education in a western democratic society is to help prepare students for their vocation, as well as for their role as citizens. A cursory review of college and university vision statements most certainly reflects the strong commitment of higher education to vocational development. This is usually interpreted as discipline-specific academic preparation for various professions, coupled with broad education in general academic fields, such as language and math, that are necessary for most professions.

Soft skills, though prized and rewarded in co-curricular and extracurricular activities, are not often found on course syllabi, which are generally focused on knowledge-based content and assessed by tests and writing projects. As we have seen in the competency models of well-respected companies, the skills of relationship building, problem-solving, and motivation are among those competencies employers say they look for, and yet, the academic programs of colleges and universities rarely teach them as they do an academic or technical competency. While many businesses have extensive HRDs, well-articulated competency models, strong performance appraisal systems, and effective coaching and training programs, most do not. Most employers depend on the higher education system to deliver a pipeline of new employees who will have the skills they need to succeed.

A few years ago, one of the authors met with a group of practicing engineers and engineering professors to discuss ways they could promote the teaching of soft skills in university engineering programs. It is a problem for the profession, because engineering curricula are so challenging that there is little room for electives or any additional courses. Like many Science, Technology, Engineering, and Mathematics (STEM) fields, engineering attracts intelligent people who are good in school and are very committed to getting the science right. However, most jobs in engineering require more than that. Engineers need to be able to influence others to their point of view, to work on a team, to present their ideas and projects in clear and appealing ways, and to communicate information to others who may not have their level of expertise.

As the group discussed this dichotomy, one hiring manager for an engineering firm exclaimed, to general agreement, "That's why I try to hire baseball players! They have learned a lot about teamwork and communication and hard work!" Ironically, next on the meeting's agenda was to find ways to attract more women to the engineering profession— and the irony of hiring baseball players was not missed. These employers wanted diversity and leadership skills, but they had no language to express what they sought or a reliable way to identify it in potential candidates that could be applied equitably.

It is not uncommon for hiring officers to admit that they often select students for interview based on the extracurricular activities—team sports, student government, and so forth—and not just what is presented on a transcript. This paradigm of the *well-rounded scholar* is passed on to students through high-school guidance counselors who encourage extra-curricular activities and sports as ways to get into the college of choice, and through career counselors in colleges who advise this as a good way to land to the best jobs. While students do indeed learn a lot from these experiences, there are two problems with this approach: First, it is often difficult to verify the actual attainment of soft skills in these activities, and second, for many students, participation in extracurricular activities is just not an option.

The traditional college student is becoming harder to define, as incoming college freshmen are less and less homogeneous. The U.S. population is aging and becoming more diverse, and higher education can no longer assume that the norm will be 18-year-old residential students dependent on their parents. Statistics from 2012 showed nearly 60 percent of all undergraduates were *post-traditional*, which was defined as older than 24 years, financially independent, working full time, or a member of the military or his or her spouse. Nearly half of these post-traditional learners had dependents, and 26 percent were single parents.[1] Although there is some evidence that this percentage has decreased with the strengthening economy in recent years, this group, which is expected to continue to surpass traditional student enrollment, is less likely to participate in school-based extracurricular activities that have been tied to soft skill attainment.

Recognizing that soft skills are often developed in settings outside the traditional classroom, many universities are adopting systems to award competencies that are attained through a variety of pathways, including service work, elective courses, and other experiences. These competencies are often represented by digital *badges*, which are machine-readable credentials that reflect competencies that have been demonstrated. Students earn and display their badges on social media and via portals such as Credly, Mozilla, and other Open Badges partners.

The Education Design Lab[2] is one non-profit that is attempting to bridge the competency development gap between higher education and the workplace. The lab has targeted micro-credentials (credentials that are earned more quickly than degrees, such as badges and certificates), 21st century skills (another name for cross-cutting soft skills), and alternative career pathways to help education and the workforce identify and communicate soft skills. The organization developed a framework of badges that include the competencies of *initiative, creative problem-solving, inclusion and equity, oral communication, catalyst, critical thinking, collaboration,* and *empathy.* Several university partners in the Education Design Lab offer one of these badges to students, and as of 2018, more than 80 badges have been distributed at George Mason University, University of Arizona, Bay Path University, Vassar College, Georgetown University, and other partners. Although this project is small, it is one of many collaborative or independent initiatives that universities are exploring to add verifiable life competencies to the university experience. In Chapter 4, we will take a deep dive into two university programs that have made these soft skill competencies central to their program mission.

Many university programs, especially pre-professional programs such as teaching, nursing, and business, stress that both classroom and supervised internships are places for students to demonstrate and informally develop professionalism and other non-cognitive competencies. In other academic disciplines, university professors often model and encourage professional competencies in academic relationships, but often, these professors do not feel comfortable giving students non-academic feedback (which is often subjective) in a knowledge-based academic course. Especially in more traditional residential institutions, faculty expect that students will come to college with certain personal and interpersonal competencies learned in the home, in high school, through social relationships, in extracurricular activities, and in part-time job experience. When students have not developed these competencies, faculty are often unable to articulate, assess, teach, develop, and communicate these competencies, especially when they are not training students for a specific career.

An example of this stress happened a number of years ago in a university where one of the authors taught. A student who was majoring in history and had excellent grades came for advisement. He had decided he wanted to be a high-school history teacher. His major professor from the history department indicated that he knew the content, could write well, and was shy. In advising appointments at this particular university, advisors were mentally armed with a competency model of sorts: a list of professional skills and attitudes that were used to assess all aspiring teachers in the program. Within minutes, it was apparent that the student had a long way to go to develop some of the competencies important for a teacher. He did not make eye contact, spoke in a barely audible voice, did not make casual conversation, and seemed reluctant to express his goals. When these observations were shared with him, he agreed that those were behaviors he typically exhibited. The author asked him how hard he was willing to work to develop the *withitness* (a quality described by educator Jacob Kounin in his theory of classroom discipline) needed to manage a classroom of adolescents. This discussion led to an investigation of other possible careers, and the student indicated he was more interested in being an archivist, a career where his current soft skills—attention to detail, organization, and strong writing skills—would be more suited. He had chosen teaching because he thought it would be easier to find a job, but he was not passionate about it, and indeed seemed fearful of the prospect. Naming a few of the competencies he would need to develop helped him decide to go with his first career choice. Without the language of competency, most advisors would have been at a loss if he had indeed wanted to develop the needed competencies. What was missing that would have helped the situation was a strong, well-defined competency model with a method to assess and develop the behaviors he would need if he did decide to become a teacher.

Higher education and business often expect that the other will fill the soft skill gap. Many professors continue to expect that job experience will include mentoring from bosses and coworkers who will teach them the expectations of the workplace and help them develop the competencies they need to succeed. But, experience shows that this is often not the case. In most workplaces, even those with sophisticated talent development departments, there is limited training in the non-cognitive skills and relatively poor coaching from supervisors or mentors who are not trained for it. Employers are much better equipped to train the technical competencies, and they, in turn, expect students to come to the job with the soft skills they are looking for.

Why Soft Skills Matter Now More than Ever

A 2017 report by the *Chronicle of Higher Education* entitled *The Future of Work*[3] describes a trend that has been ongoing in the United States since the 1970s—manufacturing has declined from 40 percent of all jobs to fewer than one in 10—and the trend is on pace to continue. Indeed, farming, fishery, and similar jobs will continue to decline; jobs that require post-secondary certificates, bachelor degrees, and graduate degrees will continue to increase. STEM fields are ascending, and with that, the need for employees who can demonstrate competence both in current technologies and in the underlying *soft skills* that position them to grow and adapt to multiple changes in their roles and responsibilities over the course of their careers.

In a 2015 review of job postings, which gives a real-world peek into the job market, Burning Glass Technologies[4] found more and more jobs are asking for baseline or soft skills. As many as one in three requested skills could be classified in this way. Burning Glass differentiates soft skills from hard skills as those baseline abilities that can include communication, writing, organization, and broad technical skills like math, as opposed to the hard skills that are unique to an occupation or industry, such as engineering or medicine. Many soft skills correspond to those competencies assessed in employee evaluation processes such as those at Dell, Disney, and others mentioned in Chapter 1.

In STEM areas, competence in the hard skills has been represented by a certification or degree, but competence in the soft skills that allow employees to adapt to changing environments has rarely been taught or measured during the educational process in the fields of STEM. The stereotypical socially awkward scientist is *not* the STEM professional many companies are looking for. Perhaps, this is why we are seeing an overabundance of employer requests for competence in teamwork, relationship building, and leadership. Writing, communication, and organizational skills are prized in every field for which Burning Glass has data. Increasing automation of lower-level processes has made it easy for everyone to perform many routine, repetitive technical skills. But, those competencies that cannot be automated—interpersonal and leadership skills, for example—are more and more sought after.

A 2016 report entitled *2026 The Decade Ahead: The Seismic Shifts Transforming the Future of Higher Education*[5] chronicled some shifts that are already happening in higher education. In response to a 2010 survey by the National Research Council, many universities reported teaching the 21st century skills of teamwork, creativity, and problem-solving. What has been termed the *T-shaped student* is becoming a goal. In this model, the vertical stroke of the T represents deep content knowledge in the academic discipline or industry, and the horizontal stroke represents the universal competencies that are prized across all industries and disciplines, such as the ability to work with all kinds of people and to think critically and creatively.

One example of how universities are embracing the T is Michigan State University. They have incorporated this model in all their undergraduate programs. According to Jim Lucas, Assistant Dean of Global Education and Curriculum at MSU,

> ...the T-model states that students need to be able to span the boundaries of disciplinary structures—artists need to work with economists, environmentalists need to work with policy makers, and urban planners need to work with medical professionals. In addition, students must be able to apply their knowledge into multiple systems not only to better understand the complexity of modern problems, but also to be prepared to adapt professionally in the new workplace.[6]

Although the name is relatively new, the underlying concept of the *T-shaped* individual has existed historically both in higher education and in the workforce. Since the emergence of the modern university in the 19th century, liberal arts or general education was shorthand for the kind of cross-cutting skills it was believed that all educated persons should exhibit. In hiring, managers have long looked for what was termed people skills and the ability to get along with others. During the industrial age, secondary educational attainment was actually a sort of shorthand that told employers that the individual could be patient, reliable, punctual, and show attention to detail[7]—all competencies that were extremely important to the workers of the 19th and 20th centuries. When hiring college graduates, employers of the last two centuries could be assured a certain level of knowledge across disciplines, as well as the ability to read critically, conduct research, and write clearly. Even more importantly, the degree represented a social network peopled by only a very few—less than 5 percent—of the most elite individuals in society. Often, this combination of competencies, together with the ability to follow direction and attend to detail, provided the basis for a successful career.

But no longer. The combined force of globalization and advancement of technology have done two things to impact higher education and the workplace. First, it has increased the speed with which a job changes, rendering the qualities of creative thinking, teamwork, learning agility, and communication more valuable than ever before while lessening the time granted to attain them. Second, it has opened global competition that must rely on verification of competency. The old social networks from college attendance are still valuable, but in a world where a graduate in St. Louis may be competing for a job with a person from Mumbai, the ability to demonstrate and visualize competence is at least as important to both the graduate and employer. Fortunately, both educational systems and workplace systems have something strong to contribute to building a future in which students can emerge from a variety of educational providers (traditional and non-traditional) with baseline and non-cognitive competencies that will form the foundation for lifelong learning in both the workplace and in continuing higher education experiences.

How Can Universities Respond?

The idea that American higher education must respond to economic, political, social, and even geographic realities is as old as the university. However, this tradition has persisted alongside an equally influential and sometimes conflicting idea that colleges and universities must maintain traditions established in the medieval universities of Europe. This dedication to scholarship at the expense of vocation, to elitism as opposed to egalitarianism, is a conflict that often slows change in non-profit and public institutions of higher learning today. Proprietary institutions and community colleges have long been unabashedly vocational in nature, setting up a dichotomy that many flagship public and private institutions have clung to in an attempt to avoid the taint of the high-profile unethical practices of some for-profits, or the perceived lower prestige of community colleges. Employers do not always realize these conflicting traditions, nor do they always appreciate that over the last two centuries, despite countervailing forces, the United States' colleges and universities have been moving in an uninterrupted path toward vocationalism and broader access.

In colonial times, American universities were decidedly English, as were the majority of cultural norms in the colonies.[8] Nevertheless, over time, they took on their own flavor because of the makeup of the social and cultural context—early western inhabitants of the American Colonies were far from their motherland and less influenced by the ideas of Europe. Harvard University, which became a template for most of American higher education, was founded to train both ministers and public officials—roles that were not seen as too far apart at that time when many European settlers had immigrated to form communities based on their unpopular religious beliefs. But, almost from the beginning, new ideas were disrupting this model. By the late 1700s, universities were taking ideas from the German model of professional academics and the scientific method, and professional schools for military and engineering were developing.[9]

The idea that higher education was attainable by more than just the elite proliferated as the new nation was being built. In 1790, America's universities had fewer than 1,000 students (all white males); 80 years later, there were 63,000 students, including some women and African Americans.[10] Throughout this time, curriculum was becoming specialized and organized into subfields such as statistics, physics, chemistry, economics, and sociology. Technical colleges, such as the United States Military Academy at West Point, centered on math and engineering, and graduates went on to build the railway system and open the mining and manufacturing industries that eventually led to the industrial revolution.

Higher education both fueled industrialization and was transformed by it. Harvard University introduced reforms in the organization and management of universities that reflected the specialization of the industrial model—the academic specializations, course and credit hour calculations for degrees, large lectures in timed sessions, and standardized grading systems that are the hallmark of higher education today, many generations past the industrial age.

As more people went to college (up to 16 percent of the population in 1940),[11] curricula related to various vocations increased. Teacher's colleges, vocational colleges, and professional schools were established. By the early 20th century, trades like business, agriculture, and journalism became academic disciplines as more careers in those areas emerged. Junior colleges began to teach automotive mechanics, commercial art, and practical nursing.[12]

In 1944, the Servicemen's Readjustment Act, colloquially known as the GI bill, ushered in a whole new era of post-secondary education. Nearly half of America's 15 million veterans participated, and higher education doubled its prewar enrollment. And, this moment impacted more than just the veterans who attended in the years following the war. According to Cohen and Kisker, "the belief that everyone could go to college became firmly established in the minds of the American people; college was no longer reserved for an elite few."[13] Indeed, the authors of this book are both beneficiaries of the GI bill—one who was educated in the U.S. Coast Guard and then able to use veteran's benefits to pursue graduate work, and another whose father was a first-generation college graduate and PhD because of the GI bill; the economic, social, and educational impact of that benefit has led to three generations of family members with graduate degrees.

In the last 60 years, universities have continued to expand in size, number, specialization, enrollment, and expense. As higher education has responded to changing demands of the workplace and of society, much of the reform has been additive—a new program and process coexists beside another that is no longer as useful. Structural changes are now taking place in the education industry that are disrupting this model. The walls between work and school, vocation and avocation, training programs and universities, and personal and professional competencies are falling down.

What educational innovations will bridge the gaps between what employers need and what higher education delivers?

One such bridge is competency-based education (CBE). This educational approach entered higher education in the United States in the 1970s and focused primarily on adult degree completion programs. Several well-known programs at Alverno College, DePaul University's School for New Learning, Empire State College, Excelsior College, and Thomas Edison State College were developed in the 1970s and 1980s.[14] The CBE model resurfaced in the 2010s as several factors began to influence higher education—reduction in financial support from states and the subsequent increase in student loan debt, greater demands for accountability from the federal government and from consumers, and an increase in adult students who need more flexible learning options.[15] There are many definitions of this approach, but according to Dragoo and Barrows, "students progress toward degree completion by demonstrating, through competency-based assessments, what they know and can do."[16]

Although implementation of CBE models can be challenging, interest continues to grow. In spring of 2014, 52 United States universities were offering or beginning to offer competency-based programs.[17] By the fall of 2015, 600 university CBE programs were in the sustained delivery, design, or initial implementation phase.[18] This approach offers a unique opportunity to students and employers to address the challenge of assessment and development of soft skill competencies.

One innovative model of teaching competencies for life is taking place at the University of California San Diego (UCSD). UCSD is a public research university located in the La Jolla neighborhood of San Diego, California. Established in 1960 near the pre-existing Scripps Institution of Oceanography, UCSD is the seventh oldest of the 10 University of California campuses and offers over 200 undergraduate and graduate degree programs, enrolling about 22,700 undergraduate and 6,300 graduate students.

To remedy the continuing lack of soft skills leadership and management competency training in most undergraduate and advanced STEM degrees, the UCSD College of Extended Studies created a unique certificate program targeting scientists and engineers from local companies whose career ladders now include leadership roles. Called the *Executive*

Perspective for Scientists and Engineers (EPSE), this comprehensive program requires classroom participation one day a week over a nine-month
period, and features a competency-based curriculum emphasizing exceptional leadership and management savvy in business roles.

The university has adopted a well-researched commercial model and
matched its curriculum with 18 leadership competencies correlated with
success in corporate roles at the director level (Table 2.1).

Students are introduced to the EPSE competency model through a
survey-guided development experience, that is, a 360-degree survey. Each
student solicits online feedback from boss, peers, and direct reports on a
complete leadership and management competency set. Feedback includes
average ratings and ranges for each competency, as well as written comments organized into three areas: (1) participants perceived leadership and
management strengths, (2) perceived developmental areas, and (3) any
other helpful advice. Complete feedback reports, with summaries to help
interpret the reports, are distributed in class. Faculty then engage in a
virtual coaching cycle that discusses competency choices, provides developmental feedback, and ultimately, results in a comprehensive development plan to address key weaknesses in the context of the participant's

Table 2.1 UCSD EPSE

EPSE instructional module	Business competency addressed
Negotiation	Conflict management
Presentations	Presentations
Leading change	Leadership identity ♦ Influence ♦ Change agility
Emotional intelligence	Relationship building ♦ Sensitivity ♦ Assertiveness
Root cause analysis	Problem-solving and decision-making
Team building	Team management
Finance	Financial acumen
Sales and marketing	Business systems thinking
Employment law	Talent management
Team building	Team management
Merging cultures	Global thinking
Strategic management	Strategic thinking ♦ Visioning
Power and politics	Diplomacy

current role and future career plans. This plan must be vetted with the participant's boss back in the workplace.

Conventional classroom instruction by a series of experts in each of the competency areas provides necessary cognitive knowledge; then, students are divided into teams and assigned work projects to apply that knowledge.

As a final test of competence at the program's conclusion, the 30 EPSE students are re-organized into three new teams and assigned senior leadership roles in a computer-based, full-immersion business simulation. The three new competing teams must then form, storm, norm, and perform as the senior leadership in a fictitious global pulp and paper business. Aggressive overall financial goals are presented as each team leads and manages the business over a five-year cycle, accelerated to the three days of the simulation. Tactical decisions are made by each role in every annual cycle, and teams must also decide on major investments in a series of risky strategic capital expenditures. This capstone event provides a practice field not only for strategic leadership competencies like *strategic thinking, business systems thinking,* and *financial acumen,* but also the interpersonal competencies of *communications skills, influence,* and *conflict management.* The computer model provides feedback on a balanced scorecard dashboard that addresses finance, associate engagement, customer satisfaction, and operational efficiency measures. Peer feedback is used to provide soft skills evaluation in competency areas like *communications* and *influence.*

As we will explore in Chapter 4, this is just one innovative way universities are striving to address soft skill competency attainment.

The challenges of the 21st century economy have placed the vast U.S. educational system and business and industry in a unique position. While both have a history of adapting to economic forces, neither has a track record of working closely together to address those forces. The differences in terminology, structure, and assessment of competencies have proven a challenge that some institutions of higher education and companies are stepping forward to bridge.

Questions for Reflection

- What are some of the major forces that are shaping the workforce of this generation?

- What kinds of workers will the employers of the future seek when automation has transformed the workplace?
- How has American education responded to social and economic challenges in the past?
- What are ways industry and education could work together to address the economic challenges of automation and globalization?

CHAPTER 3

Measuring and Developing Competence for Life

Measuring Soft Skill Competencies

Not too long ago, one of the authors attended a panel discussion session at a large national conference. The panel focused on communicating and verifying competencies learned in higher education. One panel member, a dean of a large and well-respected STEM program, commented that "you can't assess soft skills." What was even more surprising was that none of the other panelists or the moderator seemed to disagree. This illustrates the fact that, while leaders in higher education believe in the absolute importance of soft skills for success in job and life, they have resisted incorporating these important skill sets into curricula, often with the defense that they cannot be measured, and if they cannot be measured, they cannot be taught. Skillsets like *communications, problem-solving, relationship building,* and *influence* have often seemed to lack the hard edges necessary for classic grading schemes, even though these grading schemes themselves are often subjective and inconsistent.

Higher education leaders outside of business colleges may be unaware that the problem of assessing soft skills has been an issue of life or death for large corporations for many years. Confronted with the marketplace reality of survival of the fittest, and the resulting imperative to measure and predict success in key organizational positions (especially leadership roles), industry has long been able to successfully measure soft skills in a way that predicts job success. More than 50 years ago, AT&T, borrowing techniques first tried by the U.S. spy agency OSS (now CIA), began a grand experiment, and created industry's first *Assessment Center*, a set of simulations designed to test managerial candidate's readiness to assume leadership roles. The ultimate application for these AT&T Assessment

Centers was a better selection methodology for front-line leaders, an extremely important role in any organization. AT&T began with a now classic, and often cited, experiment, the Management Progress Study.[1] This longitudinal double-blind study of 422 young managers at AT&T is unique in research history. *"Probably no other personnel research study in American industry has been so well conceived and executed over so long a period of time."*[2]

The creative design, rigor of evaluation, fire-wall between assessment center ratings and any operational use, and the decades-long tracking of the participants as they percolated up the talent ladder at AT&T continues to define this as a unique and seminal study. The Management Progress Study created a best practice measurement methodology that is referred to as an *assessment center.* It also introduced and validated a differentiating set of competencies that has persisted over decades. Included in this set are familiar names like *organizing, planning, decision-making, communications, interpersonal relations/ sensitivity,* and *adaptability.*

What Is an Assessment Center?

Although it sounds like a place, an assessment center is actually a process that includes research-based elements. Well-run contemporary assessment centers are built using the same ingredients as the original AT&T centers. These include:

1. Valid criteria (e.g., competencies derived from a job or competency analysis) that can be reliably observed and measured. These include competencies that one of our authors calls *The Big Six,*[3] which are:
   - Formal and informal communications skills
   - Problem-solving and decision-making
   - Organizing and planning
   - Relationship building
   - Influence (leadership)
   - Drive or energy

2. A mixed set of simulations or exercises that replicate typical situations that a participant might see on the job, such as:

- Group meetings or conferences
- Multitasking or multiple, competing priorities exercise (presented as an in-basket or inbox)
- One-on-one situations like selling, or investigating, or confronting poor performance
- Formal and extemporaneous presentations; public speaking
- Written exercises (respond to requests for quotes, letters, e-mails, memos, etc.)

3. Facilitated by multiple trained assessors
   - Formal training in assessment center theory and history, competencies measured, exercises, and rating methodology
   - Multiple assessors for triangulation
   - An expert facilitator to lead and manage the process

4. A prescribed methodology for standardized and objective presentation of exercises and rating methodology
   - Tested and standardized exercises with scoring guides if possible.
   - Defined rating scales and required proficiencies, for example, a five-point behaviorally anchored rating scale to differentiate candidate performance
   - A method to resolve rater differences
   - A formal data integration session to ensure a complete and thorough presentation of candidate evidence and to allow independent ratings

5. Personal feedback to each participant.
   - A transparent process that engenders credibility
   - Final ratings and written feedback that highlight a participant's strengths and opportunities
   - Formal development plans

The Assessment Center Research Group, a group of Assessment Center experts and practitioners, drawn primarily from the ranks of the Society of Industrial and Organizational Psychologists (SIOP), has maintained a current set of guidelines and ethical considerations that provides more detail on definitions and process.[4] The guidelines were endorsed in 2008 at the 34th International Congress on Assessment Center Methods in Washington, D.C.

Because of the robust research history in all facets of the assessment centers, the process has been well established in industry as a legitimate diagnostic process used for both selection and development. Assessment centers are run in hundreds of companies and used for selection, succession planning, training, and development.

However, only a few universities have adopted the methodology and run centers that comply with professional standards and ethics.

Typical Assessment Center

Other chapters will describe in detail the Assessment Centers used at several academic institutions, but it is difficult to visualize an assessment center unless you have experienced one. To help clarify the process, here is an example of one individual's experience as a participant in an Assessment Center at a large, national, retail organization:

Crystal Powers started as a stocker at an ACME Hardware store in Tucson, Arizona, but quickly moved up the ranks to assistant manager in the garden department. After two years in the job, after expressing an interest in becoming a store manager, receiving above average performance appraisals, and obtaining her associate degree in business, Crystal's HR business partner encouraged her to apply to the company's management Identification Development Program (IDP). The HR partner explained that this program was used to identify and develop management talent in a proactive way. She was warned that selection into the store manager position might mean relocation, but at this stage in her career, Crystal was actually eager to see a little more of the United States.

Crystal applied, and after an interview with HR and her store manager that zeroed in on her motivations to move into management, she was accepted into a program that put her on the waiting list for the company's next Acme IDP assessment center. She was given a link to the portal on the company's intranet that provided an orientation to the program. There she learned that Acme employed a classic assessment center to help determine internal candidate readiness to manage an Acme store.

The orientation further explained that she and 11 other store manager candidates from her district would most likely travel to Phoenix, where the company ran the Southwest Area centers. The orientation previewed the program by letting Crystal know that she would be participating in a one-day series of simulations designed to emulate life as a store manager. These exercises would measure Crystal's proficiency in the task and relationship skillsets necessary to lead and manage a store. These skillsets included competencies such as formal and informal communications, ability to handle multiple competing priorities, decision-making, interpersonal skills, and leadership ability. She could expect to be involved in exercises, including group meetings, speeches, handling the typical administrative load of a store manager, and one-on-one meetings with employees.

Within a few weeks, she was notified that her center had been scheduled. Crystal Googled "Assessment Centers" and found an abundance of information on what she might expect. This helped ease her anxiety somewhat as she made the three-hour drive between Tucson and Phoenix the day before the center.

Acme had arranged an informal reception at the hotel for participants that night, and Crystal met her fellow candidates, all of whom had driven or flown in from southern California, Nevada, and Utah. The center staff dropped by for brief introductions, and she was somewhat surprised by the participant–staff-ratio—there were seven staff members for the 12 participants!

At 8:00 sharp the next morning, Crystal, her fellow participants, and the staff all met in a plenary session in the hotel's conference facility. The program administrator (a senior HR professional) had staff and participants formally introduce themselves, and then provided an overview of the program.

Crystal learned she had been assigned to a team of six for the day. The facilitator explained that this was the optimal size for a problem-solving group. Three staff members were designated as evaluators for her team. *The assessor staff consisted of a current store manager, a district manager, and a senior learning and development professional from Acme's headquarters in Dallas. Crystal learned in the orientation that the operators had both been through this program several years before, and all the staff had gone through a training program to prepare them to serve.*

She was reassured to see that her team of six was a diverse mix of Acme store associates with a similar company tenure. The two teams of six would operate in parallel during the day in separate rooms. She was given last-minute advice that acknowledged the nervousness that each participant felt, and was encouraged to stay focused on the task at hand, not worry about her performance from exercise to exercise, keep an open mind, and stretch herself (but be herself) as she engaged the exercises.

The administrator then introduced a fictitious context for the day. The fictional scenario was an imaginary retailer with a similar size, scope, and organization design as Acme, but in a different business—general merchandise and groceries. Crystal guessed this might help level the playing field in terms of any content knowledge or experience differences across participants. But, she knew that retail was retail, so there were many, many transferable challenges.

Once the orientation was over, the groups were dismissed and reassembled in their individual rooms. As promised in the orientation, the day went by in a flash. In the first exercise, Crystal was assigned to a task force and given specific problems to solve individually, and then as a group. No leader was assigned, so the group was on its own to manage time and task. The next exercise was called an "in-basket," in which she worked alone for 90 minutes to organize and decide on a jumble of multiple tasks and problems that she supposedly inherited from a previous store manager who had left suddenly and was now unavailable. After lunch, she met one-on-one with a staff member who questioned her thoroughly on her approach and solutions to the dozen or more problems she had confronted.

Next, she had to prepare for and then meet with a store associate with a performance problem. She was given the context and issue, and then met with the associate (role played by one of the staff) for

30 minutes. Crystal considered this the hardest part of the day. She knew from her real-time store experience how difficult it could be to confront and redirect marginal performance.

The day ended with another group exercise to select from among six candidates competing for a single position. First, each participant gave a short formal speech introducing his or her choice. After the six speeches were given, the group met for 45 minutes to discuss the merits of the candidates and decide on the best candidate. This exercise was much more competitive, and she noticed it exposed some behaviors not revealed in the morning's meetings. Her candidate was not chosen, but she was satisfied with the final decision.

That evening the participants were treated to a dinner out at a local restaurant, and the group thoroughly reviewed the day. It was a shared, challenging experience, so a natural bond was forming among the 12. There were many common questions. "What were the evaluators furiously writing? Did other participants get challenged on their solutions to the in-basket problems? Who 'won' in the afternoon exercise?"

The group did not have long to wait for answers, as the next morning in a two-hour debrief the administrator "pulled back the curtain" to give the participants a backstage look at all that had gone on the previous day. She revealed that each exercise was designed to trigger specific competencies. For example, the group discussions were good at revealing proficiency in communications, leadership, and interpersonal skill sets. The in-basket exercise allowed a focused look at an individual's organizing and planning skills, as well as the ability to solve problems. The role play allowed a look at a candidate's assertiveness, sensitivity, and conflict management skills. And, of course, the speeches were a chance to rate the candidate's public speaking skills.

The debrief included some company history with the process. Crystal learned that, in addition to many scientific research reports on the efficacy of the assessment center process, Acme had done its own research showing the ROI for choosing better store leaders. This was not a hard sell to this experienced group of retailers, as most of them knew the damage that could be done by a bad leader in terms of morale and talent turbulence.

The debrief also revealed the rigorous process the assessors followed in observing, recording, and rating performance in the exercises. Crystal learned that, to avoid bias, all three assessors operated independently throughout the day, each observing, recording, and rating each candidate in each exercise. They were using a five-point scale with the "three" score meaning the candidate was proficient in that competency needed by store managers. Each scale had behavioral anchors at the extremes and midpoint; these specific performance indicators ensured more objective and reliable ratings.

The two assessor teams were actually meeting separately in a different location during the debrief, and were engaged up until noon that day in what was called a data integration, or "boil down" session to share all the independent observations and ratings, and come to consensus ratings for each candidate. The assessor team focused on one participant at a time and walked through the day of exercises chronologically, sharing observations and ratings. Where there were differences among assessors, the process required resolution. The data integration methodology was rigorous and impressive. Crystal gained confidence that no matter what the outcome for her, the assessment center provided a fair evaluation, and she looked forward to the feedback.

At the end of the debrief Crystal learned she was scheduled for a two o'clock feedback session with one of her assessors. She and the assessor met privately, and Crystal first shared a rough self-evaluation that she had prepared during the debrief that morning. When the staff member revealed the consensus center ratings, it turned out Crystal had produced a similar profile, but she had actually been a little hard on herself and many of the actual center ratings were above her own.

In addition to ratings for each competency, the feedback document identified key competency strengths that Crystal would bring to the store manager role, as well as few competency areas that were opportunities for development. There was also a narrative that told the story of her assessment center experience, weaving together the exercises, her ratings, and how this would play out as a store manager.

While Crystal was warned that the Center only informed, but did not make, the final store manager selection decisions, she was pleased that her overall readiness rating indicated she could assume a store manager role in a "C" store (smaller) market when a manager role came open. As part of the formal program, each participant was also automatically enrolled in Acme's online development program, and required to put a personal development plan together, regardless of overall readiness for a particular job. Once back at work, and eager to continue to improve as a leader and manager, Crystal logged on and began her developmental journey.

As Crystal reflected on the assessment center experience, she acknowledged that she was pleased with the business knowledge she had gained with her academic degree (retail content on merchandising, retail math, and sales), but she noticed the absence in her curricula of most of the competencies that Acme found valuable in retail management—competencies that the assessment center made sure she had before she was promoted.

Crystal's experience demonstrates two strong content and process advancements in industry that might inform higher education: a more complete model of competence required for job success and a process that can be reliably used to measure that competence. Crystal's experience was transformational, primarily because it placed her in a simulation very closely aligned to realistic job challenges. She was ready to address her development areas.

Diagnosis and Prescription

The assessment center is and has been for generations an effective way to assess soft skills. To use a medical metaphor, this phase of learning might be referred to as the diagnosis. Sometimes, you are diagnosed because you recognize troubling symptoms—you are fired from a job or were overlooked for a promotion. But sometimes, your symptoms are silent—you are unaware of certain soft skills you may lack. In many cases, participants nod and agree as they receive their feedback—this is performance they have noticed or received feedback on before. In other cases, it is an *ah-ha* experience. In one assessment center for employees of a large national company, a participant received feedback that he interrupted the other participants more than 30 times in one day. After a moment of silent reflection, he said, "I am going to have to call my wife when this is over." She had been complaining that he interrupted her, but he did not take it seriously because he felt she was *nitpicking*. In an unbiased center, with assessors who did not know him but simply collected data, he was able to *hear* the feedback that he had been getting all along!

The closer the experience is to reality, the more accurate the results, and the more likely the participant is to accept the data. However, the assessment center process can be expensive. It requires payment of three to four trained assessors for each small group of six who work together for an entire day. For businesses, this is often reserved for the more high-stakes assessment—promotion to C-suite positions, or development of high-potential candidates or performers. Because of this cost, businesses often use another performance-oriented technique called the behavioral episode interview when evaluating external candidates. Once again, the principle employed is *past behavior is the best predictor of future job performance*. But, in this case, candidates are asked to self-report episodes of past behavior that prove competence in needed job skillsets. Because these are reports of behavior instead of observation of the actual performance, they are necessarily somewhat less reliable, but can still add value in diagnosing readiness for a target role. For current employees, evaluations that include surveys of coworkers, direct reports, and supervisors (360-degree evaluations) also yield helpful data concerning soft skill competency and can be a useful part of a diagnosis of current job performance.

Of course, actual job performance is more reliable than self-reporting or simulations. It is currently very popular for businesses to use the *lease to hire* process that uses staffing organizations to vet and place temporary employees to *sample* the job. Employees work for a period of time (typically months) and are assessed for specifically defined job competencies using behavioral descriptors and anchors. If the employee performs at the level expected, they can be hired; if not, their contract simply expires.

All of these various soft skill performance assessments can be used in the workplace for the purpose of selection, promotion, and development. Most universities focus solely on learning and development, and the valid assessment, or diagnosis of competencies, is a crucial first step in the development process. With few exceptions, which will be described in the next chapter, universities focus on identifying soft skills that students demonstrate through participation (not observation) in an extracurricular activity. Holding positions of leadership, planning events, and solving problems, all provide contexts for students to demonstrate, identify, and hone their competencies. However, unlike a valid assessment, this recognition does not provide a diagnosis of strengths and development areas that can lead to a prescription for growth, nor does it provide a transformational experience that individuals need to motivate them to embark on development of soft skill competencies.

Developing Soft Skills

While it is true that some soft skill competencies are strongly influenced by personality or nature, a growth mindset frees everyone to aspire to develop their soft skill competencies. Some competencies, like mountains, require a very strong commitment to attain, while others are a relatively easy climb. Employers are often unwilling to develop *steeper climbs* and use competency assessment to vet individuals before hiring or promotion. Higher education, largely, has little room to vet for soft skills because university admissions at all but the most selective institutions are driven primarily by academic achievement and test scores.

In business, one of the most popular techniques for developing these skill sets in organizational contexts is coaching based on a 360-degree survey-guided development process. Used most frequently for leadership development, the process begins with a multi-rater survey distributed by the participant to boss, peers, and direct reports. The survey typically solicits ratings and open-ended written comments and is compiled into a comprehensive report. Professional feedback reports also include norms and insightful data displays to help participants understand and interpret their feedback. But, understanding is only the first step in a three-stage process that will ensure a return on diagnostic investment. Beyond understanding the feedback, the participant must acknowledge the validity of their perceived competence and then must act to leverage strengths or remedy job or career limiting shortfalls. Understanding and acting is where a coach can be very helpful.

An integral part of coaching for developmental action involves goal-setting to address shortfalls identified in the diagnosis. And, like all goals, personal growth developmental objectives are both intellectual and emotional. To paraphrase an old adage, *the road to ruin is paved with good intentions.* Intentions can be just an intellectual exercise, but the road to developmental success is paved with true *commitment* (an emotion) to energize the behavior necessary to realize intent.

This observation was supported when the Corporate Leadership Council's research, which examined 17 different leadership developmental interventions, identified the two most impactful:

- The amount of decision-making authority given to the developing individual
- The existence of an *individual development plan*

Both are important. A development plan that is dictated by a boss or other authority lacks the personal commitment needed, especially in the face of challenging growth goals. And, a goal without a specific plan ends up being just a dream. It takes specificity and discipline, combined with commitment, to realize goals.

Preconditions to Development

A recent example from a failed leadership development plan observed by one of the authors highlights two essential personal preconditions to successful development.

In this case, the CEO of a mid-size engineering firm was experiencing morale and turnover issues among the senior leadership team. The situation reached a head when a senior leader approached the Chairman of the Board (a risky political move that highlights the severity of the problem) to report the difficulty, and to warn of possible additional turnover ahead in key roles. The CEO was confronted by the Chairman, and an external leadership development firm was engaged to help. A diagnosis was conducted (a 360-degree survey and personality inventory) and a senior coach assigned.

The diagnosis revealed a clear and classic leadership profile. The CEO's leadership strengths were very distinct: *strategic thinking, financial acumen, assertiveness,* and *business skills* all surfaced as key assets. Likewise, developmental opportunities were also clearly identified: *self-awareness, relationship building, active listening,* and *sensitivity* were all below the norm. It was the archetypal dichotomy: a smart, business savvy leader with a clear task agenda, but lacking the ability to build relationships; he was unable to engender the necessary trust and commitment from his team. The CEO had superior intellectual capacity (IQ), but lacked interpersonal competence (EQ).

After a two-year development plan failed to bring about the needed changes, the CEO was dismissed. An autopsy on the process confirmed that the CEO never really did accept the need to change, nor did he truly commit to working on his action plan. In other words, he was not *coachable.* As affirmed by research by Leslie and Van Velsor at the Center for Creative Leadership, "the typical leadership development assumes the executive 'gets it' and wants to change."[5] Yet, the research indicates that most derailed executives, even in the face of strong contrary evidence, are confident that what worked for them in the past will continue to work in the future. *They are simply not motivated to alter their behavior,* even in the face of dismissal.

Three steps must be taken to assure successful leadership development. The first is a general sincere awareness of the need to grow—a desire to improve. Once that step is taken, the second is a motivation to act on the identified needs ("what's in it for me?"). The third necessary step is a skill-building plan.

Elements of Good Development Plans

Once openness to change and personal commitment to this change have been tested, then the final step toward change is a good development plan. A successful plan requires the following elements:

1. It must be based on a solid assessment of strengths and weaknesses. This assessment must be personal and objective.
2. It must exist in an organizational context. The plan includes elements that will develop the performer and the organization in which the performer works.

3. It must be focused on one or at most two changes.

4. It must include actions and experiences that teach the most (i.e., challenging projects, developing a mentor, and other on-the-job experiences).

5. It must be staged and dynamic: it needs near and distant horizons (six months, one year, and three years) and must change with context.

6. It must have buy-in support and ongoing involvement of the performer's supervisor.

Coaching Through the Process

A good development plan has much in common with a good personalized lesson plan. There is diagnosis of learning needs, feedback, and a personalized learning plan. This process is based on decades of educational research in the field of andragogy, a word that is based on the Greek words for man (andra) and leader (agogus), and literally means leading adults to learn. In the field of andragogy, the role of this *learning leader* is transformed—the teacher is a coach.

The role of coach is that of a facilitator who guides learners through a process of understanding.[6] This includes building awareness of self through behavioral assessment and feedback, practice, modeling, mentoring, cognitive coaching, and action planning. Coaches work in corporate settings, as individual contractors, and increasingly, in the context of education, taking on the role that was previously held by an instructor. It is said that, instead of a *sage on the stage*, a coach is a *guide on the side* of the learner.

When U.S. public schools emerged and flourished in the 19th and 20th centuries, the only existing instructional model was based on the 7th–12th century cathedral schools, which taught basic skills to young (male) children who were training to become priests. This model (pedagogy, or teaching children) became entrenched in both public and higher education in the United States. As the world wars of the 20th century led to the desire for more widespread education for adults, the methods used were still essentially those used for children. In this traditional model, the teacher makes all decisions about *what will be learned, how it will be learned, when it will be learned, and if it has been learned.*[7] By contrast, the andragogical model emphasizes the agency of the learner to develop in ways that benefit his or her other personal needs and context.

The principles of andragogy (teaching adults) differ from traditional pedagogy (teaching children) in several ways that support the assessment and acquisition of soft skills both in the workplace and university classroom.[8]

1. *The need to know*: Adults must know *why*. The initial assessment of competencies is one way that learners develop a *why* for their learning. If they see evidence of development areas in an assessment center, in their work, or life, they are more likely to develop a compelling *why* for learning.
2. *The learner's self-concept*: Adults have a deep need to be seen by others and treated by others as capable. Coaches help adults solve their own problems and develop their own competencies, demonstrating that the power for change is within them.
3. *The role of the learner's experiences*: Lindeman (1926) wrote that "experience is the adult learner's living textbook." All learning must be tied to past or present experiences. Knowles, Holton, and Swanson (2010) wrote: "To children, experience is something that happens to them; to adults, experience is who they are." An assessment validates the experiences that make them who they are.
4. *Readiness to learn*: Adults are ready to learn the things they need to know at the stage of their life where they are now. Readiness to learn can be created by transformative experiences, such as simulations, feedback, exposure to superior performance by others, and individual coaching.
5. *Orientation to learning*: Adults are not subject-centered; they are life-centered, or project-centered. Development should include application to real-life situations.
6. *Motivation*: Adults are motivated by some external pressures, but most significantly, by intrinsic pressures such as job satisfaction, self-esteem, and quality of life. Competency development includes references to these motivators and promotes the self-esteem and quality of life of the adult learner.

Skillful coaches use all these principles in their interactions with adults who are developing soft skills. The assessment diagnosis creates the need-to-know, and often, the motivation to grow. They encourage those they coach to practice soft skills in the workplace and to self-assess their effectiveness. After a successful coaching relationship, clients (or students) will feel able to coach themselves as they continue to develop the skills they will need in future roles and organizations.

Final Thoughts on Developing Soft Skills

While sometimes more challenging than acquiring a technical skill, learning to be a better communicator, decision maker, or team player can be learned in the service of being a better employee and leader. The first step, of course, is learning exactly which competency is important in the career and life context. Common definitions, articulated behaviors, and strong assessments leading to personal coaching are the next steps toward a lifetime cycle of self-improvement.

Questions for Reflection

- What is meant by the term soft skills? What is meant by the phrase often repeated in organizations that *we hire for hard skills, but then have to fire for soft skills.*
- Describe the classic assessment center. Name at least three of the required elements to meet the expectations outlined in Assessment Center Standards and Ethics.
- Measuring soft skills requires a process that is both reliable (can be replicated) and valid (actually predicts future behavior). Discuss how assessment centers meet these requirements.
- What was the Management Progress Study, and what made it so unusual?
- Describe what is meant by a *survey-guided leadership development process.*
- What are the key considerations in a successful developmental experience?

CHAPTER 4

Embracing Competency for Life: Two University Stories

Academic programs that rigorously assess and intentionally develop soft skills do exist, and many more are in early stages of implementation. In this chapter, we highlight two very different programs in traditional institutions that have made the transition from saying they teach soft skills to actually assessing and developing them. In both cases, these are not individual programs, but reflect philosophies of competency that are interwoven into the fabric of the entire curriculum.

Alverno College in Milwaukee, Wisconsin

Chartered in 1887 as St. Joseph's Normal School, Alverno became Alverno Teachers College in 1936. Alverno is historically and still predominantly a college for women. It adopted its current name in 1946. Alverno offers weekday and weekend undergraduate programs, as well as a Master of Arts program for teachers and business professionals, an MBA, and a Master of Science in Nursing. The Weekend College was opened in 1977 as the first alternative timeframe program in Milwaukee to serve working women in the area. While the baccalaureate degree programs and residences are still open only to women, the graduate degree programs are open to both women and men. Alverno uses an abilities-based curriculum and narrative evaluation, rather than a letter or number system for grading.

As far back as 1973, Alverno had asked the question, *Wouldn't it be great if a university actually helped you learn the process skills it takes to successfully practice the knowledge you gain in college classrooms?* They then boldly set out to build a unique program to do just that.

Now, almost a half century later, students who register at Alverno not only receive classic instruction in their chosen discipline, and are awarded degrees in business, engineering, and nursing, but they are also taught and evaluated in the competencies necessary to *successfully apply* that knowledge in the world of work. At the heart of this learning process is a general competency model applicable across disciplines, coupled with an extremely sophisticated assessment center.

At the assessment center, and in selected classroom evaluations, each student strives to reach required levels of proficiency in each of the following competency areas:

1. *Communication*: Alverno graduates make meaning of the world by connecting people, ideas, books, media, and technology. They demonstrate and master the ability to speak, read, write, and listen clearly, in person and through electronic media.

2. *Problem-solving*: Alverno graduates define problems and integrate resources to reach decisions, make recommendations, or implement action plans. They demonstrate and master the ability to determine what is wrong and how to fix it, working alone or in groups.

3. *Social interaction*: Alverno graduates can facilitate results in group efforts by eliciting the views of others to help formulate conclusions. They demonstrate and master the ability to elicit other views, mediate disagreements, and help reach conclusions in group settings.

4. *Effective citizenship*: Alverno graduates make informed choices and develop strategies for collaborative involvement in community issues. They demonstrate and master the ability to act with an informed awareness of issues and participate in civic life through volunteer activities and leadership.

5. *Analysis*: Alverno graduates are independent and critical thinkers. They demonstrate and master the ability to use experience, knowledge, reason, and beliefs to form carefully considered judgments.

6. *Valuing*: Alverno graduates approach moral issues by understanding the dimensions of personal decisions and accepting responsibility for consequences. They demonstrate and master the ability to recognize different value systems, including their own. They appreciate moral dimensions of their decisions and accept responsibility for them.

7. *Developing a global perspective*: Alverno graduates understand—and respect—the economic, social, and biological interdependence of global life. They demonstrate and master the ability to appreciate economic, social, and ecological connections that link the world's nations and peoples.

8. *Aesthetic engagement*: Alverno graduates integrate the intuitive dimensions of participation in the arts with broader social, cultural, and theoretical frameworks. They demonstrate the ability to engage with the arts and draw meaning and value from artistic expression.

These eight competencies are the Alverno College faculty's statement of what a liberally educated student should be able to *do* with what the knowledge they have gained.

Mastering these eight core abilities is what gives an Alverno graduate the power to stand out from the crowd.

Dr. Georgine Loacker (1926–2013) was the first chairwoman for the Alverno Assessment Council. Dr. Loacker was instrumental in establishing the competency model and assessment process as a *way of life* at Alverno, not only as an integral part of student growth and learning, but in other areas as well. New faculty, for instance, are assessed on these competencies using an in-basket exercise and simulated faculty meeting as part of the hiring procedure.

Alverno has heavily invested in their version of Competency-Based-Education through dedicated physical facilities, including rooms set up for group roundtable discussions complete with observer's stations, projection rooms and carrel, audio- and video-recording and playback equipment, and two-way mirrors. All these enable a thorough and complex assessment of competencies for each student at intervals throughout the college experience. An important point about the elaborate system of competency assessment is the focus on development. This entire sophisticated process is designed not just for evaluation, but more importantly, to facilitate feedback and support for developing the specific competency.

Alverno draws its competency assessors from advanced students, faculty and staff members, alumnae and members of local business, and professional and volunteer communities. Assessors from the community enhance the process, as they often represent the business or profession being sought by the student being assessed. This improves the credibility of the evaluation and demonstrates to the student the importance of the process.

Despite nearly 50 years of successfully employing CBE, the Alverno model has been slow to catch on. They attribute this to the tremendous effort needed to set up the program. Although there is growing interest, Alverno remains unique in dedication and sophistication.

> "Alverno has always been ahead of its time,
> starting with its trailblazing assessment and
> competency-based learning model. This prepares
> a woman to be a self-aware professional who is
> primed to quickly ascend into leadership roles.
> The big picture is the only picture at Alverno."[1]
> KOSOVKA SPRECO, Class of 2016
> Human Relations Analyst,
> Briggs & Stratton

> "Words cannot describe what Alverno does for
> women. As alumnae, we are community pillars and
> have the courage to work as active citizens because
> we learned to engage in productive dialogue and
> together confronted important topics. You can't be
> an Alverno woman and be passive."[2]
> ELLEN HOPPER, Class of 1996
> Chief Operating Officer,
> Northwestern Mutual Wealth Management

An Alverno Story: Laura McMillan

Let us explore the Alverno CBE difference more thoroughly through the personal experience of one graduate, Laura McMillan. Laura obtained both her BS in Business Finance and her MA in Instructional Design Technologies and Adult Learning from Alverno. Now in the midst of a very successful career, Laura is currently the Vice President of Training Development Programs for Instructional Technologies Inc., an industry leader in innovative transportation safety and operations training based in Vancouver, Washington. Instructional Technologies features online training lessons, virtual simulation technologies, and a learning management system. Their focus is an industry that employs a high-risk audience: transportation workers, specifically professional drivers and warehouse personnel.

Laura grew up in Indianapolis, but her father's job relocation brought her to rural northeast Wisconsin. The move to rural life was a bit of a culture shock, but she eventually became a fan of life along Lake Michigan, and is now a permanent resident of the Badger State. When it came time to *shop* for a college, she knew she wanted return to a large city and she chose Wisconsin's largest: Milwaukee. Milwaukee provided numerous college options, including University of Wisconsin-Milwaukee and Marquette University. Laura wanted to check out Alverno College, a small private, women's college on the south side of town. The idea of attending a private women's college was appealing, given that Laura had only attended public schools. Also attractive was Alverno's reputation for quality and value. Laura had decided on a pay-as-you-go strategy for her education to avoid any debt. To her, college was an investment, and she wanted the best return. So, she added Alverno to her schedule while in Milwaukee with her father to scout universities.

Both University of Wisconsin and Marquette met her expectations, but Alverno immediately exceeded them. There were many surprises as she explored the Alverno campus. She was charmed by the neighborhood surrounding Alverno. The college was nestled in the trees of a Milwaukee suburb that reminded her of her childhood neighborhood. The college has since expanded, but then there were only three main buildings: one that housed the library, chapel, and all the classrooms; a second that housed the dorm; and a third that was living quarters for the school's Sisters of St. Francis. Additionally, there was the Alverno Elementary school and day care, which, Laura later learned, was a bit of a *petri-dish* of a school for kids using a pedagogical version of Alverno's curriculum. Also of interest was Alverno's weekend college program, and internships that began in the first semester, regardless of your chosen major.

She was also attracted to Alverno by the low instructor to student ratio (1:10) and perhaps the biggest innovation, the *ability-based* (competency) curriculum, which, when explained to her, seemed intuitively obvious. The Alverno staff explained the science behind the curriculum and visiting alumni became real-world examples of the success of the Alverno way of doing things. Although she had her SAT and ACT scores in hand, the admissions counselors did not seem particularly interested. They were more intent on explaining the assessment process to her, and how that would be used to identify her strengths and developmental needs. The Alverno *matrix* concept (eight competencies, each with four levels of proficiency) was a little overwhelming at first, but it quickly made sense.

She learned that, in addition to knowledge gained in her chosen major at the assessment center and in selected classroom evaluations, she would be held accountable before graduation to reach proficiency in each of the following competency areas:

1. Communication
2. Problem-solving
3. Social interaction
4. Effective citizenship
5. Analysis
6. Valuing
7. Developing a global perspective
8. Aesthetic engagement

After application and acceptance, one of Laura's first experiences at Alverno was an initial assessment of her proficiency in the eight Alverno competencies. This assessment center included videotaped speeches, role plays, and participation in group problem-solving. The process was somewhat nerve-wracking, but she knew this was a baseline assessment, and that she would be supported in her future development.

Laura had not settled on a major when she arrived at Alverno, but was considering education or business management. She began her coursework in secondary education, but a freshman internship at a Milwaukee High School allowed her to test this major immediately in a realistic work context. She quickly decided that she could not see herself teaching in this setting, but, prophetically, a friend told her that she had a knack for teaching, and that no matter what career direction she took, she would end up in training.

She ultimately chose a business management major in finance, with an arts and humanities minor. She later reflected that the persistent approach of always putting her learning *in context* was one of the key advantages to her education. Doing an internship as a freshman (as opposed to the more common practice of doing it as a senior) allowed her to sample her major in context early on, and actually resulted in a dramatic change in major. And, as a further reminder of the ultimate application (context) of her business degree, the ability-based (competency) approach was woven into each course, and each lesson. For every academic experience, there was a tie-in to a relevant competency.

When course syllabi were provided at the beginning of each semester, there were no scheduled midterms, or even periodic quizzes. With no tests, how would instructors know how well she was doing? She quickly learned that the college relied solely on the assessment center activities conducted at the end of every semester to assess content acquisition and proficiency in application. The activities involved self-feedback plus instructor or assessor feedback. The centers emulated real-world situations where Laura would have to apply her new knowledge more spontaneously, so preparing for a center was like preparing for life at work—get a good night's sleep, have a hearty breakfast, and come in ready to work.

Later, she compared her college experience with friends who attended UWM and other larger schools. She heard stories of how students gamed the academic system by paying others to produce essay papers, or sit in for them to ace an exam. The assessment center made that impossible under Alverno's competency-based system. You, and only you, were required to show up and *apply* course content in a practical setting immediately following instruction. Alverno had elevated the axiom "knowledge is power" to "*applied* knowledge is *superior* power." So, Alverno was guaranteeing to future employers a truly proficient business finance expert with all the soft skills, too. She later learned this is why business leaders in Milwaukee often remarked how competent Alverno grads are and how readily they assumed leadership roles.

After getting her baccalaureate, Laura entered the banking industry. She obtained her stock broker's license and excelled at trading stocks and bonds. When her boss hired summer interns to do lead-generation work, Laura gravitated toward a training role. She created a *Brokerage 101* course that was quickly successful and adopted office-wide. She could also sense straightaway that she was applying all the skillsets she had learned at Alverno, which not only included her financial acumen, but initiative, communication, problem-solving, analysis, valuing, and social interaction.

She moved up to a company that had just innovated the concept of *online trading*. The ROI value of online trading required that customers participate in online trading, thus reducing the cost of accessing a live broker. While her peers were a bit threatened by sharing (and giving up) this capability, Laura jumped in, learned the new system, and began training customers. She had to overcome her peers' objections to *technology taking over their jobs*. When Laura re-framed the fear into an opportunity to discuss clients' portfolios versus just the transaction of trading, they recognized the value and were willing to accept the technology. Laura took the risk of learning the technology and showed her peers how to use it and how to train clients with confidence. It was not until the retail brokers embraced the technology and were willing to teach clients how to use computers, access the Internet, and place trades that Internet trading really took off and the company attained their ROI goals. The net effect was a win–win. The company's net assets boomed and clients were empowered by this new technology.

With this success in hand, Laura was asked to work on developing customer training programs and broker training programs at a regional level and soon thereafter, a national level. Laura still had her day job as a brokerage consultant, but her role expanded, and Laura found she really enjoyed teaching others how to manage their own finances, essentially empowering them to take control of their financial destinies. Laura saw how the competency skillset acquired at Alverno gave her the communications, problem-solving, and interpersonal savvy to succeed.

Around this time, Laura was contemplating a master's degree. She considered law or an MBA, but neither really excited her. She soon realized how much she enjoyed the training work and getting involved in curriculum design. Her work experiences confirmed for her that Master's in Education was what she should pursue next. It never occurred to her to attend any school other than Alverno.

The Master's program at Alverno co-mingled K-12 teachers, administrators, and adult workforce trainers like Laura. The Master's program was also ability-based. A unique feature of the program was that it revealed how Alverno constructed the undergrad programs and assessment process.

After graduate school, Laura shifted industries and joined a large, international trucking and logistics company. In her new role, Laura applied her communication skills using teams from across the company to help analyze and redesign work processes. Originally, Laura was challenged as to why she was getting blue-collar involvement (including drivers), but the quality of her work product ultimately justified her inclusive approach. Her Alverno ability skillset had become her natural approach.

Laura's success throughout her career highlights some of the implicit advantages to the Alverno approach. Beyond the technical knowledge she gained in business and education, and even beyond the Alverno *matrix* of competencies and proficiency levels, something else happens to the Alverno graduate. Laura's assessment experiences, the reinforcement of competency application, and continuous feedback also provided these key outcomes:

- *Self-confidence*: Successive achievement in the assessment centers engendered a belief in self, which leads to greater confidence, being proactive, taking risks, and achieving results.
- *Life-long learning*: Constant feedback and growth also created in Laura a desire for continual and life-long learning. Implicit in the Alverno approach was a recognition that an individual cannot know everything, and instills a mindset to involve and learn from others, and an attitude for community learning.
- *Leadership*: While leadership was not an explicit Alverno ability, each assessment center required the Alverno student to assume a leadership role. They were required to orchestrate decisions and deal with implications on the *mock* teams they led. Although assessment center activities are simulations, the not-so-subtle effect is that students learn that not only can they apply knowledge, but they can lead others, too.

Once again, while not necessarily explicit learning objectives, these are very positive outgrowths of learning the Alverno way. All this helped with the transformation that Laura personally felt, and that she has since learned that other Alverno graduates feel, too.

Laura's experience in education and knowledge about how Alverno constructs their curriculum for the different disciplines has also reinforced how ingeniously the competencies translate into tasks, activities, discussions, and lectures that are woven into any vocational field. They happen to work for both kids and adults, too. Alverno's eight competencies can stand on their own and are contextualized quite easily. From Laura's perspective, everything about the competency model's relevance to real-world results is valid.

As stated at the outset, Laura now works for a company that has created a comprehensive platform for safety training. Whenever Laura engages clients on creating a curriculum for their crews, she begins with an approach reinforced by her education, *begin with the end in mind:* the results that leadership is trying to create (or avoid). Laura now works with clients to determine what the key performance indicators (KPIs) will be and then set about discussing how performance happens: the combination of knowledge, skills, behaviors, and attitude needed to perform the job. So she considers the circle complete. Just as she learned how Alverno's eight competencies were required for career and life success, she ties her client performance objectives into the competencies required to realize them.

Lipscomb University in Nashville, Tennessee

Lipscomb University is a private faith-based coeducational institution with a strong focus on undergraduate education in the liberal arts and sciences. It began in 1891, when two men, David Lipscomb and James A. Harding founded the Nashville Bible College in Nashville, Tennessee. In many ways, they were innovators in education—their college was created not to train ministers, but lay people who wanted to integrate faith and academic excellence into their careers. Lipscomb and Harding admitted both men and women as students, which was unusual for a bible college at that time.

In 1903, the college found a permanent home at the 110-acre farm of David and Margaret Lipscomb, in what is now the urban Nashville community of Green Hills. In 1918, the school was named David Lipscomb College in honor of one of its founders and the donor of its property. By 1988, the school had begun to develop its reputation as an excellent institution not only for liberal arts, but also for professional majors such as education, accounting, and pre-med. To reflect this growth, it was renamed Lipscomb University. Today, Lipscomb is classified by Carnegie as a research doctoral institution and has more than 4,500 students in programs including engineering, technology, entertainment and arts, nursing, pharmacy, theology, education, and many other fields. The university awards bachelors, masters, and doctoral degrees. In 2017, Lipscomb University was ranked as a national university in the annual U.S. News and World Report's *2017 America's Guide to Colleges*. Lipscomb debuted on the list at 176, thus joining the ranks of the nation's top universities.

Toward the end of the 20th century, Lipscomb began offering night classes for working students. This program grew with the establishment of the College of Professional Studies (CPS), which focused on programs for working adults. CPS was initially envisioned as an incubator for innovative programs that would respond to workplace needs, provide innovative learning experiences, and anticipate changes in the higher-education landscape. In 2013, CPS began experimenting with the use of assessment centers to evaluate incoming students on 15 competencies from the following competency areas:

1. Conceptual
2. Communication
3. Leadership
4. Interpersonal
5. Personal
6. Management

This program was named CORE—customized outcome-based relevant evaluation. In December 2013, the Southern Association of Colleges and Schools Commission on Colleges (SACSCOC), Lipscomb's accrediting body, granted the school permission to award credit based on these competencies demonstrated in the CORE assessment center.

Since then, Lipscomb has been at the forefront of regional and national efforts to address the needs of adult learners using competency-based education. In 2014, the Council for Adult and Experiential Learning published a case study on Lipscomb's CORE assessment program, the first of a series on emerging models in CBE (Council for Adult and Experiential Learning 2014). Lipscomb is a founding member of the Competency-Based Education Network (C-BEN). Additionally, Lipscomb was approved in 2015 to participate in the Federal Experimental Sites initiative to investigate ways to deliver competency-based learning using federal financial aid.

Unlike Alverno, Lipscomb's CORE competencies are each related to a specific electronic badge and academic course. The process begins with a baseline assessment in the CORE assessment center, which uses simulated work situations to measure a student's competencies. Three or four trained assessors who meet accreditation requirements as university faculty observe the student's performance as they work independently in groups of six to respond to the typical challenges of a day at work. Following the eight-hour assessment, the assessors meet together to integrate the data they have collected and score the students on a scale of 1–4, with 4 indicating the level of a strategic leader and 1 indicating an elementary beginner. To achieve undergraduate credit, the student must attain an applied level 2 badge. This indicates that the student can perform the competency at the level of a first-level supervisor. Graduate students are expected to earn badges at an advanced level 3 or strategic level 4 in order to earn graduate credit.

Badges are awarded based on the following levels:

Talent pipeline equivalent	Proficiency level	Credit awarded	Description of competency proficiency
Strategic leader	4 strategic	Graduate credit	Demonstrates mastery of competency and is capable of mentoring and coaching others in its application.
Functional manager	3 advanced	Graduate credit	Demonstrates expert application of competency and is capable of coaching others in its application.

First-level supervisor	2 applied	Under-graduate credit	Demonstrates advanced competence and is capable of modeling this competency for others.
Individual contributor	1 elementary	No university credit	Possesses the fundamental knowledge, skills, and motivations needed for this competency; can consistently apply this competency.
	0 inadequate	No university credit	Falls short of the knowledge, skills, and motivations needed in this competency for role. Development is needed to reach the required standard.

Undergraduate students who do not show applied level 2 competency in the initial assessment center can enroll in a credit bearing course, which includes online learning modules, job-embedded activities, practice sessions, and coaching designed to develop the competency in a realistic environment. While students can earn up to 30 hours and 15 competencies in the assessment center, the Bachelor of Professional Studies degree requires all students to show competence in six of the 15 areas—communicativeness, influence, drive and energy, relationship building, organizing and planning, and problem-solving and decision-making. So, although the assessment center is a form of credit for prior learning, for most students, it is also a baseline assessment upon which future learning is built.

Following the assessment, the student works with a trained coach to design a personalized plan to develop competencies identified in the assessment. The student then enrolls in competency development courses in addition to other university requirements, such as general education requirements and major area courses. In the competency courses, the student works with the coach to develop the competencies, at the student's own pace, using competency-based online modules.

The coach is a fully credentialed faculty member with specialized coaching training. The coach serves as a *thinking partner*, helps the student set goals, holds the student to his or her plan, listens to the student, asks thought provoking questions, gives reflective feedback, and points to resources that may be available to help the student reach his or her goals. The role of the coach is different from the role of a traditional faculty member. The coach does not assess; assessment is done by a centralized team in the assessment center. The coach does not set deadlines; the learner is in charge and is allowed to set the pace. The coach does not give assignments; the coach helps the learner choose assignments from a modularized online toolbox to develop each competency. The coach does not assign grades; the learner passes when she or he successfully demonstrates the competency on a final authentic assessment that is evaluated by trained assessors.

Lipscomb's College of Professional Studies offers undergraduate and graduate degree programs. In these programs, not only are the soft skills developed, but academic and technical competencies are learned as well. In all courses, students have a choice of two rates of learning—one is a six-month subscription that allows students to work on some competencies very quickly and take their time on others and the other is an eight-week course that allows flexibility in timing during the course as long as all the learning activities and final assessment are successfully completed within the eight weeks. This flexibility in timing is especially helpful for post-traditional students who have outside schedules to consider during an academic term.

A Lipscomb Story: Jamie Cage

Nashville native Jamie L. Cage Jr. is a graduate of Lipscomb University's College of Professional Studies, where he earned a Bachelor's of Professional Studies in Organizational Leadership with a concentration in Human Resource Management. Jamie served eight years in the Army National Guard and was a Yellow Ribbon Post-9/11 G.I. Bill scholarship recipient at Lipscomb. He has worked in human resources (HR) in various capacities, and for the last four years, he has been a workday techno-functional consultant with multiple large companies in Tennessee and D.C. Currently, he is working as an independent consultant program manager at Nissan North America's headquarters in Nashville, where he and his team are building a digital HR presence.

Jamie's decision to go to college was, in his words, "an accident, divinely aligned." He was a very young HR manager for the State of

Tennessee Child Support Services. In that role, he was delivering a training for Operation Stand Down, a program to translate military service into academic equivalency. At the end of the presentation, the Dean of Veteran Students at Lipscomb, who was also a board member for Operation Stand Down (a non-profit dedicated to services for veterans in middle Tennessee) approached Jamie. She said, "You have to come to Lipscomb. We need people like you—people who not only want to be professionals, but people who are already professional." Jamie, who had not considered going to college, was intrigued, especially when he learned that he could get credit for competencies he had already developed on the job and in the military.

> Ultimately, that changed the trajectory of my life. I went from a $13.00 an hour job to a highly paid professional career because of the lessons I learned and the relationships I developed at Lipscomb. The support from staff, mentoring from faculty, and comradery with the other students helped me to a whole new level.

Largely because of his army leadership training and work experience, Jamie excelled in the assessment center, earning 30 credit hours in one day, the maximum credit allowed. That, combined with other credit received in the military, helped him complete his undergraduate degree in a little over two years. Some of his strongest competencies are organizing and planning, relationship building, influence, and problem-solving and decision-making.

> Knowing my competency strengths has helped me sell myself in every job I have had. I have it on my resume and on my LinkedIn account. I can explain to people that I not only have the HR knowledge I need to help them improve their companies, I also have the interpersonal and leadership skills that will help me implement the change that they want to happen at their companies.

Just what did Jamie learn about himself in that assessment center experience?

Fear. I had no idea what the grading criteria were, no idea what the right answer was. I learned I could walk in that fear and perform anyway. One of the other things I learned was about diversity and inclusion. My Assessment Center had men, women, black, white … and I felt I was being judged on my performance, not on anything else. Not my background or how much I studied the night before. I felt that what I had learned through my [life] experience was valued.

Because he earned all of the competencies assessed in the assessment center, Jamie was able to focus most of his course work on other competencies that are embedded within the specific courses he took. These included HR technical competencies, mission focus, coaching, and marketing, which continue to help him as he markets himself as an independent consultant. But just because he earned credit in 15 competencies does not mean he did not continue to learn about them and hone them. "I use every single one of those 15 competencies every single day. I now know how to define them, to develop them, and to communicate them to my colleagues and supervisors."

Today, Jamie is a gifted HR practitioner, public speaker, and HR architect. He is committed to diversity, inclusion, and education, and has developed a passion for public service and for the field of HR. Jamie specifically focuses on learning management, training and development, HR implementations, competency-based training, and the architectural structure of HR. As of 2018, Jamie was also pursuing CSM, MBTI, SHRM-SCP, PMP, and SPHR certifications.

After his graduation in 2016, Jamie returned to Lipscomb University to pursue a Master of Professional Studies degree in Organizational Leadership with a concentration in competency-based design, so that he can create competency-based learning in his own business endeavors. Some of the competencies Jamie attained as an undergrad were actually on the graduate level (3s or 4s on the assessment scale), and so, he began his master's degree with six credit hours already earned. He was able to build on those competencies to take his leadership to a strategic (C-suite) level. In the future, Jamie plans to earn a DBA and teach at the university level, even if it is only on a part-time basis. "I need to do things for myself, but

I also need to do things for others to feel fed. I want to help others like I have been helped through education and mentoring."

Another Lipscomb Story: Madeline Doe

Madeline is a student with a somewhat different story. Her real name and certain details are masked at her request to preserve her privacy. She dropped out of school and moved out of her parents' home in 2012 when she gave birth to her son. With no support from the child's father, she began processing checks in the back office of a regional bank, where she received excellent performance reviews and regular pay increases, so that she is now at the top of her pay scale. In 2017, her son started school himself, and Madeline felt it was time to do something to ensure her family's future, and to achieve the goal, she had had to put off several years before. Madeline wanted to be able to tell her son that she finished college, and to be an example for his educational aspirations. After four years in the bank with increasing responsibility in the operations side, she wanted to pursue customer service and management—jobs that required a college degree and leadership skills.

Madeline chose Lipscomb because a friend told her about the assessment center and how it could reduce the time and cost of a degree. She thought it would be an opportunity to get credit, as well as a way to learn more about her leadership abilities and development areas. She had always been a good student and was confident that her work experience would help her do well.

However, after the assessment, she was a bit disappointed that she only earned nine hours in the center, and that she still had three of the six required competencies to develop: communicativeness, influence, and relationship building. In her initial feedback session, the assessor told her that her habit of sitting back quietly and letting others make the decisions while she did behind-the-scenes work was not going to lead her to the competencies needed for a management position in her company. She needed to learn strategies to communicate clearly and completely in writing and in speaking and to develop ways to influence people to consider her ideas. Social communication and greater assertiveness would be helpful in building the relationships necessary for leaders and team members.

Madeline met with the advisor who would work with her throughout her career at Lipscomb. In their first conversation, they discussed her baseline assessment, her learning and career goals, and the pace at which she would like to work on her degree. Initially, Madeline wanted to accelerate her learning because her son was in school and work was slow. However, the holidays were a busy time at work, and her son had a school break, so she estimated that she would need to work at a slower pace in December. Together, they set pacing goals that accommodated these various needs. She would have to take three different types of courses: a few remaining general education requirements, technical competencies in her concentration area of business, and the leadership competencies identified as areas to develop.

Madeline enrolled in her first group of competencies and worked at her own pace through the online modules in general education and in one of her leadership competencies, communicativeness. As she already knew (from the assessment center and other formative assessments) exactly what her current level of communicativeness performance was and where she needed to be, she and her coach could decide on the online modules that would give her the information and practice she needed to succeed. This assessment information guided everything she did as she worked to attain her goals. The CORE courses she took each had the following components:

- Regular coaching conversations: Her development coach used cognitive coaching techniques and questions to help Madeline build a personal sense of self-efficacy. She learned that she could improve her own performance in the future as she gained more experience and leadership responsibility. She practiced integrating and applying the information she learns in her personal and professional life, so that she can continue to do that even when she no longer has a coach.
- Toolbox of online learning modules: A series of personalized learning modules provided learning activities, including formative assessments that Madeline could complete at her own pace and in the context of her own job.

- Mentoring: Madeline's coach helped her identify a mentor at work who can give her honest feedback in the context of her job.
- Practice sessions: Madeline participated in synchronous online practice sessions where she interacted with other students who were working on the same competencies. Sometimes, students observed each other and gave feedback: at other times, her coach observed the group and provided feedback.
- Job-embedded experiences: Madeline needed to learn how to implement her competencies in the context of her own professional and civic life. With the help of her coach, she set personal challenges for herself and carried them out in the context of her job, and in one case, at a homeless shelter where she volunteered. She asked her mentor and coworkers to complete a behavioral checklist to share with her that gave her feedback on how she approached the challenges. Her coach helped her reflect on the experience and the feedback received.

When Madeline and her coach thought she was ready to be reassessed on the leadership or personal competencies she was working on, she completed an online behavioral assessment. Some of these re-assessments (influence, for example) are taken in a simulated work setting with a group in a virtual meeting room online. She demonstrated the competency at a level 2, so she earned three credit hours toward her degree and a digital competency badge. She also had business competencies that were assessed with a case study, and some general education competencies that required multiple choice exams and some written projects.

Madeline is on the path to graduation, though she will not finish in two years like Jamie did. Regardless, she will be learning valuable skills that could move her into a more fulfilling and rewarding job. She is learning how important competencies like relationship building and influence are to her professional and personal life, and how she can continue to grow throughout her career.

Alverno and Lipscomb serve as models for redefined CBE, but are by no means examples of typical competency-based education programs in the United States. Indeed, they are outliers, in that they emphasize soft skills and that they tie competencies for life to the curriculum through assessment and credit. Other programs, such as Loyola of Chicago, are in the initial stages of implementing assessment centers and leadership competency models into the curriculum. Many other institutions are investigating ways to tie extracurricular activities to competencies and to communicate those experiences through badges and competency transcripts. There are many paths to be explored, and innovative universities are forging paths that others can travel.

Questions for Reflection

- What are some similarities in the Alverno and Lipscomb models? Why do you think these programs both were developed in private institutions?
- How do the two programs differ in their approach? In what ways do those differences meet the needs of their particular clientele?
- Imagine the possible barriers to implementation in programs such as these in other traditional institutions and public institutions.
- Contrast the Alverno or Lipscomb experience with your own undergraduate education. What are the major differences?
- What role should competency models and competency assessment play in addressing the soft skills gap?

CHAPTER 5

Working Together to Close the Gap

Higher education recognizes the need to develop in their students competencies that will lead them to successful careers. At the same time, employers have a need to develop in their employees those competencies that are necessary for efficient daily operations of their business organizations. Both educational institutions and organizations that employ their graduates share the need to provide training and development to address these common interests, particularly in the hard skills of technical and functional ability. Now, more than ever, economic and social forces require that these pathways be extended to address universal, non-cognitive soft skills as well.

Both employers and higher education can and often do find innovative ways to work together to meet their mutual needs of developing the competencies that students need for a successful career and that employers need to run their organizations effectively. Now, more than ever, economic and social forces require these relationships to be extended to create pathways for all students to develop universal non-cognitive soft skills as well.

Higher Education and Organizational Talent Development in Transition

Higher education and workplace are obviously linked in many ways. First, of course, higher education itself is a workplace, employing close to four million people in the United States alone.[1] Second, many fields such as education, health care, law, and engineering directly depend on undergraduate or graduate institutions to train entry-level certified employees in their profession. The vast majority of employers, however, simply require a college degree—on the assumption that employees will come to the workplace with personal qualities and valuable baseline skills that will allow them to be easily trained for a particular role in the organization.

Despite this interdependence, higher education and organizations that hire graduates historically have had little more than surface interaction. While many employers and universities collaborate to provide internships, hiring fairs, and collaborative partnerships, they do not often share valuable curricular expertise or communication-specific competencies needed for various roles in the workplace. Indeed, in many cases, collaborations between the schools that produce graduates and organizations that hire them have been seen as a conflict of interest—universities maintain their independence, attempting to keep the curriculum pure from the influence of the corporate world, and many hiring organizations disparage the educational process in higher education, maintaining that only the workplace can provide the real-world experience needed to succeed. The organization of most universities makes collaboration even more difficult—the general skills are taught in silos in many different departments by specialists who may know their own fields, but are largely unaware of how their discipline and other disciplines may interact in the workplace. Many university educators do not know about the advances in HR corporate training over the last quarter century, or how the research in training and development can impact academic curriculum and teaching methods.

This attitude is changing, however. Over the last 60 to 70 years, higher education interest in workplace competencies has grown dramatically. After the Second World War, when thousands of veterans began flooding the nation's universities, schools began to see the first wave of post-traditional students and the need to provide academics that connected to the workplace. More recently, other pressures on higher education have emerged. There has been a political and economic push to increase higher education attainment rates. The knowledge economy requires a more diverse workforce with higher levels of education, and key to this is college completion for adult learners. Students now come to college with a diversity of learning preferences, modalities, and past educational experiences. As the traditional student demographic wanes, the post-traditional has grown, making up a majority of all undergraduate students in recent years. Post-traditional students are more likely to demand a return on the investment of their college experience—expecting to get better jobs and higher pay as the result of the knowledge and skills they attain. Indeed, as college costs rise, even parents of traditional-aged students are demanding that their investment lead to a lucrative career.

Higher education recognizes that university libraries and experts no longer have a monopoly on information dissemination or verification. Online credentialing organizations and alternative education providers such as boot camps and massive open online courses (MOOCs) have proliferated. Employers and students have a variety of options to learn new skills. Universities must both compete and uphold quality standards in accreditation environments that limit their ability to be as agile as non-credit-granting organizations. To compete in the marketplace, universities are beginning to recognize that they must teach students in ways that support the self-efficacy and life-long learning that is required in our rapidly changing society. Educators are leaning into their role as mediators of learning, instead of dispensers of information, and are recognizing that the viewpoint and expertise of corporate and non-profit practitioners have an important place in higher education.

With the unemployment rate declining, the number of adults returning to school for undergraduate and graduate education has leveled off from recession-era enrollments. Individuals are finding jobs, perhaps low-skilled jobs, but they reduce the amount of time adults have to pursue education, even when they know they need it for long-term viability in the marketplace. This force is encouraging universities to seek partnerships with employers to build enrollments while meeting the employer's needs for a more competent workforce. This trend will likely continue, as traditional-age enrollments decline. Economists predict a 10 percent decline in 18-year olds by 2029, a demographic force that has universities considering ways to diversify their student pool.[2]

Higher education institutions are not the only ones feeling the crunch in the new knowledge economy. Increasingly, companies and other hiring organizations are discovering they cannot fill all of their own training needs. According to *ATD Research: 2014 State of the Industry*, organizations spend an average of 1,208 U.S. dollars per employee on training and development and offered an average of 31.5 learning hours a year.[3]

And, the nature of that training and development is changing. According to Bersin, employee learning is one of the most rapidly changing HR functions.[4] Digital platforms, MOOCs, competency-based learning, and micro-learning modules are swiftly being integrated into the learning centers of large companies. Employees have less and less time to learn—as few as 20 minutes a week—which is about the length of a TED talk video. Bersin cites a study by Deloitte Consulting LLC[5] that reviewed corporate training and assessed employee satisfaction with it, finding that most employees are dissatisfied with their company's learning systems, and that frequently what is learned is not retained. Additionally, many larger companies have huge learning systems that are so complex that employees feel they do not have time to navigate them to find the learning they need. Technical and informational learning (new regulations, systems, and practices) can take more than the available time to provide, even while HR professionals are facing employee issues that are more relational than technical. With large and well-funded HR departments that are struggling to keep up, the nation's nearly 60 million employees of businesses with 500 or fewer employees[6] are unlikely to receive the comprehensive training it takes to succeed in an economy that requires fewer transactional and more relational skills.

The future seems even more daunting in a 2017 study by Rainie and Anderson on the future of jobs and training, conducted by the Pew Research Center and Elon's Imagining the Internet Center. In non-scientific polling, researchers canvassed technologists, scholars, practitioners, strategic thinkers, and education leaders on their opinions about the likely future of workplace training. A strong consensus of these experts was that there will be many millions fewer jobs for many millions more people in the future. According to many respondents, automation and the trajectory of ever-more sophisticated technology will eventually make the workforce irrelevant, even in what are now high skilled jobs such as lawyers, insurance adjusters, and accountants. The experts agreed that, in the next decade, training and learning systems will not be able to adapt fast enough to prepare people for the 21st-century economy.[7]

Despite the dire headline, the Pew respondent's answers held some hopeful themes. First, they believed that innovative training ecosystems will emerge with the use of online technologies, augmented reality, and hybrid or real-world classes. Organizations will expect employees to learn continuously, and universities will diversify and innovate to meet workforce needs. Second, they believe learners will cultivate 21st-century skills through apprenticeships and mentoring, and that creativity, adaptability, and critical thinking will be more valued. Finally, new credential systems such as badging and certificates will be developed to quantify self-directed learning and other non-traditional ways of acquiring competence.[8]

These themes are hopeful, and large employers are already investing in learning management systems, sophisticated online technologies, badging ecosystems, and mentoring programs. However, the vast majority of employers, as we have seen, do not have extensive human resources training and development (HRD) budgets to support these innovations. Collaborations with universities can be one way to achieve employee learning targets for lower costs and higher yields.

Examples of Employer Partnerships for Competence for Life

Most universities that have adult degree completion or business college programs have long histories of workforce partnerships. The following examples come from just one of those programs, Lipscomb University, where soft skill competencies form the basis of the fully online competency-based undergraduate program in organizational leadership, and several graduate certificates and master's programs in leadership.

Lee Company

Lee Company, a privately held residential services and commercial contractor located in Tennessee, employs over 1,000 heating and air conditioning technicians, electricians, plumbers, engineers, construction and facilities managers, and support personnel. Lee began as a family-run company in 1944, and experienced unprecedented growth as their hub, Nashville, became one of the fastest-growing cities in the United States.

In 2017, Workplace Dynamics conducted a survey of employees of large local companies. In that survey, Lee was ranked "the number one place to work." The survey respondents reported that the company is like a family.

Do not be fooled; Lee is a highly profitable and well-managed company that prizes training and education. But, an important part of Lee's mission from the very beginning was to "create a workplace where our employees can thrive." This was evident in a unique component, the Lee Company University (LCU), which offers classes where employees can learn new skills, achieve a journeyman's credential in the trade of their choice, and expand their career opportunities. LCU hosts a graduation ceremony every year for the employees who have earned advanced certification and their families.

Lee Company's vision is to be a leading provider of professional services for facilities and homes. Out of this vision comes a culture of leadership that is manifested in programs that are rare in companies of its size. It was the dual idea of leadership and development that drew Lee Company and Lipscomb together in 2015 at an event sponsored by Lipscomb to bring local employers and higher education representatives together to discuss innovative ideas in education.

Since that time, as Lee Company was quickly growing, its need to develop leaders from within led them to license the Organization Systems International (OSI) Polaris® competency model, a commercially available model that is also used at Lipscomb University. Using the OSI model, Training and Education Manager, Corey Driggs, developed a leadership training program for high performers, emphasizing the competencies that are most needed in Lee's workplace. Driggs has worked with several local universities to provide high-quality training and coaching for his employees. In collaboration with Lipscomb, employees who show high-level leadership potential participate in the CORE assessment center, earning up to 30 hours of college credit for their performance of workplace competencies. For competencies identified as potential development areas, employees participate in group executive coaching, competency seminars, and optional online learning modules. At the end of the academy, the participants are reassessed on their leadership competencies and can earn undergraduate or graduate credit for competencies they demonstrate. They can leverage that credit toward a university certificate or degree if they choose.

Lee Company is one example of the innovation that can happen when employers who care deeply about development and training reach out to universities and partner together for universal competency. According to Driggs,

> Investing in our people through education is not only a business strategy, it is a people strategy. Creating the atmosphere where people can truly thrive is not just a catchy mission statement, it is the purpose of everything we do. Partnering with Lipscomb University is one more way we provide an opportunity for our employees to thrive.

Pinnacle Financial Partners

Pinnacle Financial Partners is a bank headquarters in Nashville, Tennessee. And, although somewhat similar to Lee in the number of employees, Pinnacle Financial Partners had a very different need—to develop the competencies of their partners (clients) instead of their employees.

The Nashville-based firm was started in 2000 by Terry Turner, a veteran of a large regional bank. Banking has traditionally been viewed as a commodities business driven primarily by price, but Turner had an idea to break away from that mold and differentiate from the competition by offering exceptional tailored services and support to its clients. According to business author Calloway, "The basic strategy was to target small businesses and their owners, which was just about the whole business market in Nashville… ."[9]

To do this, Pinnacle hired experienced, wise banking professionals with loyal clients and built an organization centered on people. When the people—the affluent clients and owner-operated businesses—were successful, Pinnacle was successful. Pinnacle professionals were always identifying and assessing client needs, and then seeking a solution that could fill this need. Pinnacle Senior Vice President and Business Banking Team Leader, Chip Higgins, and his colleagues understood the organizational problem with owner-operated businesses—often the owner and one or two employees filled all the boxes on the organizational chart. Even in larger companies, the expense of hiring experts in many functional areas is often cost prohibitive. Managers *wear many hats* and thus have to demonstrate a wide range of technical competencies. Pinnacle believed professional development for its owner-operated businesses was a solution to this dilemma, and began offering eight-week mastermind training groups for their customers and for any other small businesses that wished to join. These groups trained small business owners in areas that would help them increase their profitability. To take this initiative to the next level, they turned to Lipscomb to further develop technical competencies after the eight-week sessions were over, and to allow the participants to expose their own employees to quality professional learning as well.

Pinnacle's successful business model aligned well with Lipscomb University's mission to provide exemplary and personalized leadership development to its students and professional development partners. In 2014, Lipscomb and Pinnacle began discussions about collaboration. At the time, Lipscomb already had in place a competency-based assessment center of leadership and personal competencies, and was just implementing a competency-based online learning platform to help develop those competencies.

Initially, Pinnacle's goal was to provide small business clients with a resource to grow their own and their employee's competencies in the four areas they had identified in their mastermind groups: finance, talent management, marketing management, and operations. Over the three-year development of the project, however, it became evident that the soft skill competencies from OSI provided as much or more value than the technical ones.

In a business, soft skills run in the background of daily operations. Soft skill requirements are ongoing and diverse at the individual level. Even the best operations manual or robust strategy loses its effectiveness if the people implementing them lack personal qualities such as drive and energy, communicativeness, and relationship-building. It was apparent that development programs would need to be equally diverse and individualized.

Although the learning was designed initially to be *un-coached*, it became evident through beta testing that a coach to help participants set goals, track progress, and celebrate success would be a huge added value in the technical, interpersonal, and leadership competencies. From Pinnacle's perspective, the business owners or their employees must immediately apply the new learning to specific problems or gaps in their business model if they hoped to produce a lasting system or strategy in their business. With the addition of leadership and personal competencies to the offerings, the need for a coach to help participants apply them to their daily lives became even more crucial.

The main challenge was how to build in a highly relational component to a system that is essentially *on demand*. Second, the cost of a professional executive coach for entry- or mid-level employees was out of reach for most small businesses. The initial answer was to train a part-time employee as a coach, who could then provide very basic levels of distance coaching. This same employee could also serve as an administrator of the program. For more extensive coaching, businesses would have the option to purchase additional hours from an International Coaching Federation(ICF)-certified coach. While this model is not perfect, it does provide a taste of coaching and support for implementation that is missing in most online professional development.

Together, Lipscomb and Pinnacle Financial Partners developed scores of learning modules in the technical competencies and provided access to learning and coaching around the OSI Polaris® competencies as well. This provided an opportunity for owner-operated businesses and their employees to learn practical skills that also met the academic standards of a college-level course. When the project, called PinnaclePro, is complete, participants will be able to earn badges that represent the competencies they learn and demonstrate; they can earn college credit if they wish.

The Lipscomb–Pinnacle partnership is unique, in that the university and organization are equal partners and co-developers of the product. Pinnacle expertise is combined with that of university professors to create a learning experience that is applicable to current challenges and also provides an academic framework for further learning. The development experience has not been without surprises, however. In the beginning, the development phase was expected to last about one year. In reality, that became three years. Challenges with meshing the needs of two highly regulated businesses (education and banking), limited technology, and prioritization of a project that was not the core responsibility of any of the collaborators slowed the process. Nevertheless, the project demonstrates the potential to approach competency-based education from the inside-out—from a business need to an educational solution—instead of outside-in—a university producing *competent* graduates to fill organizational job openings.

Tractor Supply Company

Tractor Supply Company (TSC), headquartered in Brentwood, Tennessee, is the largest operator of rural lifestyle retail stores in the United States. Founded in 1938, the company operates more than 1,600 stores in 49 states and has more than 24,000 employees.

Lipscomb University and TSC formed a collaboration in 2014 to support TSC's leadership development program. Participants from around the United States came in for a week-long training that included a one-day assessment of universal competencies from the OSI Polaris® model. In the three years that this initial project was in place, more than 200 TSC *leading leaders* participated in a one-day assessment center. They all received individual 45-minute feedback sessions from trained assessors on Lipscomb's faculty in which their performance was reviewed in 15 competencies: *assertiveness, active listening, change agility, communicativeness, composure, conflict management, drive and energy, influence, initiative, organizing and planning, presentation skills, problem-solving and decision-making, relationship-building, results orientation, and team player.*

Although Tractor Supply chose not to work specifically with the employees to develop these competencies, the employees were instructed to share their reports with their supervisors and provided printed resources to help develop them on their own. Tractor did leverage the rich data from the assessments to identify areas in which to focus future training and to identify employees to further develop into leadership roles. Lipscomb and Tractor were able to disaggregate the data to identify the competencies that new hires were bringing, and those that were most common in employees who rose through the ranks. They could also identify which competencies were most common in which role and which ones needed further development across the organization or in specific geographic locations. This kind of information was helpful in developing more tailored professional learning experiences in response to organization needs.

Overcoming Barriers

As we have seen, partnerships between the higher education industry and corporate realm must overcome several barriers for success. Some of these are structural—universities are structured around academic disciplines that rarely correlate well to any specific industry or job role, which is the structure that makes the most sense to employers. Leaders of academic units are often not conversant with the industries whose talent they provide. Corporations are similarly illiterate in the complex governing structures of universities, and often do not know where to turn for collaboration. These barriers can be overcome by university outreach to local businesses and businesses outreach to universities that provide many of their employees.

Another barrier is communication and perception. Universities and corporations often speak different languages and have different perceptions of student soft skills. For example, a 2017 survey published by The Chronicle of Higher Education[10] revealed that 70 percent of employers felt colleges were doing a good or excellent job preparing students for the workplace. There was variation depending on the industry, however. In more technical areas such as medicine, health care, computer services, and manufacturing, 75–85 percent of employers felt schools were doing a good job. In industries that depend more heavily on soft skills—business, media, education, consumer services—satisfaction was closer to 60 percent. Employers cited communication, problem-solving, and technical skills as those they most desire, but these are not the skills they say they are seeing most often in recent college graduates.

Interestingly, in this survey, the university respondents ranked soft skills higher in importance than the employers did overall, and ranked the student's possession of those skills higher than employers did. This points out a difference in perspective that could indicate that employers are hiring entry-level employees for technical skills, and then face greater challenges down the road as they look among their workforce for leadership potential and succession planning. Higher education, with a greater emphasis on the whole student and less on immediate employability, perceives the importance of competence for life earlier in the student's development. Their perception that students have greater soft skills than employers think they do when they see them in the workplace could indicate how differently education and industry define these competencies.

Conversations and active listening between employers and educators can provide a place to broaden knowledge and leverage the expertise that the other provides. Badges and other micro credentials such as certificates can provide a way to articulate the competencies attained in the workplace and in the classroom so that these competencies can be rewarded by each entity. Universities can provide course credit through the Prior Learning Assessment (PLA) for competencies and badges earned on the job. Competency models that are already prevalent in industry can be adopted by higher education to form the structure of a competency-based curriculum.

There is also a philosophical barrier between higher education and corporate employers, with many flagship public and private institutions disparaging the academic benefit of soft skill competencies, and many employers dismissing higher education's ability to teach those competencies. As we have seen in multiple examples, higher education has and must continue to adapt to the economic realities faced by students, and consider how soft skill competencies are assessed, developed, and recognized in an educational setting. Employers must recognize the significant track record of developing leaders that American higher education has maintained for hundreds of years and reach out to partner with institutions that aim to define, assess, and develop competency for life in their students. Higher education must continue to innovate and expand the idea of general education to include competencies that will benefit the student, the economy, and our communities.

Questions for Reflection

- What can we learn from the history of higher education since the Second World War? How might this impact how employers and universities approach their partnerships?
- What are some barriers to higher education–industry partnerships? How can they be overcome?
- What are some ideas for higher education–industry partnerships that might be mutually beneficial?

Notes

Chapter 1

1. U.S. Department of Labor (1997).
2. The Princeton Review (2017).
3. Griffiths (2009).
4. Griffiths (2009).
5. Campion et al. (2011).
6. Griffiths and Washington (2015).
7. Griffiths and Washington (2015).

Chapter 2

1. Soares, Gagliardi, and Nellum (2017).
2. Education Design Lab (2018).
3. The Chronicle of Higher Education (2017).
4. Burning Glass Technologies (2015).
5. The Chronicle of Higher Education (2016).
6. Lucas (2015).
7. Reynolds (2014).
8. Cohen and Kisker (2010).
9. Cohen and Kisker (2010).
10. Cohen and Kisker (2010).
11. Cohen and Kisker (2010).
12. Cohen and Kisker (2010).
13. Cohen and Kisker (2010).
14. Ford (2014).
15. Burnette (2016).
16. Dragoo and Barrow (2016).
17. Kelchen (2015).
18. Nodine (2016).

Chapter 3

1. Bray (1964).
2. Thornton and Byham (1982).
3. Griffiths (2010).

4. International Taskforce on Assessment Center Guidelines (2009).

5. Miller (2001).

6. McGrath (2009).

7. Knowles, Holton, and Swanson (2010).

8. Knowles, Holton, and Swanson (2010).

Chapter 4

1. Alverno College (2018).

2. Alverno College (2018).

Chapter 5

1. Snyder and Dillow (2016).

2. Grawe (2018).

3. ATD Research (2014).

4. Bersin (2017).

5. Bersin (2017).

6. SBA Office of Advocacy (2016).

7. Anderson and Rainie (2017).

8. Anderson and Rainie (2017).

9. Calloway (2005).

10. Maguire Associates (2013).

References

Alverno College. Retrieved from http://alverno.edu

Anderson, J., and L. Rainie. 2017. *The Future of Jobs and Jobs Training*. Pew Research Center: Internet, Science & Tech.

ATD Research. 2014. *State of the Industry 2014*. American Society for Training and Development.

Bersin, J. 2017. "Employee Learning Enters the Digital Age." *SHRM HR Magazine*.

Bray, D.W. 1964. "The Management Progress Study." *American Psychologist* 19, no. 6, pp. 419–29.

Burnette, D.M. 2016. "The Renewal of Competency-Based Education: A Review of the Literature." *The Journal of Continuing Higher Education* 64, no. 2, pp. 84–93.

Burning Glass Technologies. 2015. *The Human Factor: The Hard Time Employers Have Finding Soft Skills*.

Calloway, J. 2005. *Indispensable: How to Become the Company That Your Customers Can't Live Without*. J. Wiley & Sons.

Campion, M.A., A. Fink, B.J. RuggeBerg, L. Carr, G.M. Philips, and R.B. Odman. 2011. "Doing Competencies Well: Best Practices in Competency Modeling." *Personnel Psychology* 64, no. 1, pp. 225–62.

Cohen, A.M., and C.B. Kisker. 2010. *The Shaping of American Higher Education: Emergence and Growth of the Contemporary System*. Jossey-Bass.

Corporate Leadership Council. 2001. *Voice of the Leader: A Quantitative Analysis of Leadership Bench Strength and Development Strategies*. London: Corporate Executive Board.

Dragoo, A., and R. Barrow. 2016. "Implementing Competency-Based Education: Challenges, Strategies, and a Decision-Making Framework." *The Journal of Continuing Higher Education* 64, no. 2, pp. 73–83.

Education Design Lab. 2018. "21st Century Badging Challenge." *Education Design Lab Homepage*.

Ford, K. 2014. *Competency-Based Education: History, Opportunities and Challenges*. UMUC Center for Innovation in Learning and Student Success.

Friedman, T.L. 2016. *Thank You for Being Late an Optimist's Guide to Thriving in the Age of Accelerations*. Allen Lane.

Grawe, N.D. 2018. *Demographics and the Demand for Higher Education*. Johns Hopkins University Press.

Griffiths, B. 2009. *Taking the Mystery Out of Talent Management: A Research Report in Support of Polaris® Competency Models and 360° Multi-Rater Measurements.* Organization Systems International.

Griffiths, B.E. 2010. *The Big Six Leadership Competencies.* Best Practices.

Griffiths, B.E., and E. Washington. 2015. *Competencies at Work; Providing a Common Language for Talent Management.* Business Expert Press.

Human Resources Planning Society. 2004. *The Power of a Development Plan.* New York, NY.

International Task Force on Assessment Center Guidelines. 2009. "Guidelines and Ethical Considerations for Assessment Center Operations." *International Journal of Selection and Assessment* 17, no. 3, pp. 243–53.

Kelchen, R. 2015. *The Landscape of Competency Based Education: Enrollments, Demographics and Affordability.* Center on Higher Education Reform, American Enterprise Institute.

Knowles, M.S., E.F. Holton, and R.A. Swanson. 2010. *The Adult Learner: The Definitive Classic in Adult Education and Human Resource Development.* Burlington, MA: Elsevier.

Leigh, A., and M. Maynard. 2003. *Perfect Leader.* Random House.

Lindeman, E. 1926. *The Meaning of Adult Education.* Windham Press Classic Reprints.

Lucas, J. 2015. "T-Shaped Professionals: A Liberal Arts Education for the 21st Century." *Undergraduate Learning Goals-Undergraduate Education @ MSU.* https://undergrad.msu.edu/news/view (accessed August 23, 2018).

McGrath, V. 2009. "Reviewing the Evidence on How Adult Students Learn: An Examination of Knowle's Model of Andragogy." *Adult Learner: The Irish Journal of Adult and Community Education*, pp. 99–110.

Maguire Associates Inc. 2013. "Survey of Employers Who Hire Recent College Graduates with Bachelor's Degrees." *The Chronicle of Higher Education and Marketplace.*

Miller, K.K., and W. Hart. 2007. *Choosing an Executive Coach.* Center for Creative Leadership, Greensboro.

Nodine, T.R. 2016. "How Did We Get Here? A Brief History of Competency-based Higher Education in the United States." *The Journal of Competency-Based Education* 1, no. 1, pp. 5–11.

Organization Systems International. *Polaris® Competency Model Development Guide.* San Diego, CA.

OSI View. 2013. "The Power of a Development Plan." *Literature Review.* San Diego.

Paquette, D. 2017. "Bosses Believe Your Work Skills Will Soon Be Useless." *The Washington Post.*

Reynolds, G.H. 2014. *The New School: How the Information Age Will Save American Education from Itself.* Encounter Books.

SBA Office of Advocacy. 2016. "Small Business Profile: The United States." U.S. Small Business Administration Office of Advocacy.

Snyder, T.D., and S.A. Dillow. 2016. *Digest of Education Statistics 2016.* National Center for Education Statistics (NCES) Home Page, a Part of the U.S. Department of Education.

Soares, L., J.S. Gagliardi, and C. Nellum. 2017. *The Post-Traditional Learners Manifesto Revisited: Aligning Post-Secondary Education with Real Life for Adult Student Success.* American Council on Education.

The Chronicle of Higher Education. 2016. "2026 The Decade Ahead: The Seismic Shifts Transforming the Future of Higher Education." *The Chronicle of Higher Education.*

The Chronicle of Higher Education. 2017. "The Future of Work: How Colleges Can Prepare Students for the Jobs ahead." *The Chronicle of Higher Education.*

Thornton III, G.C., and W.C. Byham. 1982. *Assessment Centers and Managerial Performance.* Acad. Press.

About the Authors

Nina Jones Morel is professor of education and dean of the College of Professional Studies at Lipscomb University in Nashville, Tennessee, where she developed a competency-based online program and an International Coach Federation-accredited Performance Coaching graduate program. She is a professional coach and author of two books on coaching: *How to Develop an Instructional Coaching Program for Maximum Capacity* (Corwin 2012) and *Learning from Coaching: How do I work with an instructional coach to grow as a teacher?* (ASCD 2014). She speaks and trains about competency-based education and coaching. Nina is a graduate of Lipscomb University (BA) and Tennessee State University (MEd and EdD) and has taught at the middle school, high school, and university levels. She was awarded the Milken National Educator Award for teaching excellence in 2005.

Bruce Griffiths is the founder of Organization Systems International (OSI) based in San Diego, California. His company specializes in leadership selection and development since its inception in 1980—and has been recognized many times for professional contributions, including two best practice citations from ATD for developing unique business simulations designed to teach strategic leadership competencies. Bruce is recognized as a thought-leader in competency modeling and development. He has spoken at dozens of professional conferences and published numerous articles. He is the author of the book, *Competencies at Work*, which has been recognized as an essential read in the talent management space. Bruce is a graduate of the United States Coast Guard Academy (BS) and San Diego State University (MS Industrial & Organizational Psychology). He is currently on faculty in UC San Diego's College of Extended Studies where he teaches leadership.

Index

OTHER TITLES IN THE HUMAN RESOURCE MANAGEMENT AND ORGANIZATIONAL BEHAVIOR COLLECTION

- *Creating Leadership: How to Change Hippos Into Gazelles* by Philip Goodwin and Tony Page
- *Practical Performance Improvement: How to Be an Exceptional People Manager* by Rod Matthews
- *Conflict and Leadership: How to Harness the Power of Conflict to Create Better Leaders and Build Thriving Teams* by Christian Muntean
- *Creating the Accountability Culture: The Science of Life Changing Leadership* by Yvonnne Thompson
- *Managing Organizational Change: The Measurable Benefits of Applied iOCM* by Linda C. Mattingly
- *Lead Self First Before Leading Others: A Life Planning Resource* by Stephen K. Hacker and Marvin Washington
- *The HOW of Leadership: Inspire People to Achieve Extraordinary Results* by Maxwell Ubah
- *Leading the High-Performing Company: A Transformational Guide to Growing Your Business and Outperforming Your Competition* by Heidi Pozzo
- *The Concise Coaching Handbook: How to Coach Yourself and Others to Get Business Results* by Elizabeth Dickinson
- *How Successful Engineers Become Great Business Leaders* by Paul Rulkens

Announcing the Business Expert Press Digital Library

Concise e-books business students need for classroom and research

This book can also be purchased in an e-book collection by your library as

- a one-time purchase,
- that is owned forever,
- allows for simultaneous readers,
- has no restrictions on printing, and
- can be downloaded as PDFs from within the library community.

Our digital library collections are a great solution to beat the rising cost of textbooks. E-books can be loaded into their course management systems or onto students' e-book readers.
The **Business Expert Press** digital libraries are very affordable, with no obligation to buy in future years. For more information, please visit **www.businessexpertpress.com/librarians**. To set up a trial in the United States, please email **sales@businessexpertpress.com**.